C000193882

Tiki
Cocktails

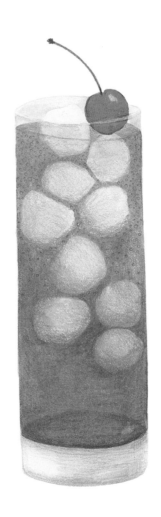

Tiki Cocktails

200 SUPER SUMMERY DRINKS

DAVID ADAMS

illustrations by HEATHER MENZIES

Smith Street Books

Contents

introduction

Who doesn't love a tiki party? Flamboyant garnishes, bright colours, ornate ceramic mugs, coconuts, pineapples, hula, Hawaiian shirts, ukuleles, fire and most importantly, lots and lots of alcohol.

The phenomenon began with a man named Ernest Raymond Beaumont Gantt, a former prohibition-era bootlegger who travelled extensively throughout the Caribbean and Pacific Islands. Gantt fell in love with the fruits, cuisines, aesthetics and cultures of the places he visited, and in 1933, he opened a tropical-themed cocktail bar in Los Angeles called *Don the Beachcomber's* – and thus the tiki bar was born. Gantt eventually changed his name to Donn Beach, and spawned a worldwide craze for potent, rum-based drinks and tropical décor.

Donn Beach was gregarious, creative, cultured and didn't mind a drink or three – a man after my own heart.

This book is full of classic and modern tiki cocktail recipes from all four corners of the globe. Stock up your liquor cabinet, juice some fruit, cut some garnishes, check the servicing date on your fire extinguisher and invite a bunch of great friends over for a night of alcohol-fuelled nonsensical frivolity.

GLASS TYPES

Tiki cocktails do what they're supposed to when you drink them from any type of vessel, but they're really not quite the same unless you have the right glassware. More so than regular cocktails, tiki drinks have produced their own specific mugs, glasses, bowls and vessels specific to the drink that goes in it.

◄ Highball glass

Your standard tall glass that comes in many shapes and sizes.

◄ Old fashioned glass

The classic short cocktail glass. Sometimes called a 'lowball' glass by mouth-breathing cretins. Good for low-volume cocktails with a high alcohol content or just good old fashioned straight whisky.

◄ Double old fashioned glass

Much like it's younger brother, only a bit bigger. As a result of its size, it holds more volume inside it. Do I really need to go on?

◀ Hurricane glass

A tall, curvaceous cocktail glass, usually with a short stem. This glass holds around 500-600 ml (17–20½ fl oz) of delicious drink. It was named after the tiki classic Hurricane cocktail (see page 23).

◀ Poco grande

Quite similar to the hurricane glass, the poco grande is the more classic-shaped cocktail glass with a longer stem.

◀ Martini glass

An elegant conical glass with a long stem, which one might see a man in a white dinner jacket sipping from in a popular series of spy movies *(although he was a flippin' idiot because you should never shake a martini)*.

◀ Cocktail glass

A long stemmed glass similar to a martini glass but a little smaller and often with a slightly rounded or flat bottom.

◀ Pearl diver glass

This rather obscure glass gets its name from Donn Beach's tiki classic Pearl Diver cocktail (page 48). It has a straight base and curves up into a bowl at the top.

◀ Swizzle cup

A tall and sexy metal cup that tapers out at the top. Great to freeze or pack with ice so it gets all frosty on the outside.

◀ Metal julep cup

Similar to a swizzle cup, only shorter, this ornate silver and pewter bourbon catcher was very popular at the Kentucky Derby in the 1800s. Although, so was slavery.

◀ Copper mug

The classic vessel for the Moscow Mule. Legend has it a man was trying to sell vodka in America at a time when people weren't overly interested in drinking it. He mixed it with ginger beer and lime juice, put it in a stout copper cup and before he knew it, people all over America were drinking vodka by the gallon.

◀ Tiki mug

Now we're getting to the good stuff. These intricate ceramic mugs are the most iconic part of the tiki craze. Based on the carved wooden heads from the islands of Polynesia, Micronesia and the Pacific, these mugs were pioneered by the father of tiki himself, Donn Beach. You can get quite addicted to buying these little monsters.

◀ Mara amu mug

One of the classic tiki mugs, named after the drink that went in it. The drink originated at the Mai Kai restaurant in Fort Lauderdale, Florida. They have a big carved wooden statue shaped like the mug. Or maybe the mug's shaped like the statue … I tried asking the statue once and it became clear I'd had one too many Mara amus (the recipe is on page 135).

◄ Ceramic rum barrel mug

Much like its name suggests, this is a barrel-shaped mug, made from some kind of ceramic. Good for putting rum into.

◄ Opened coconut

When you don't have the 'correct' glass or mug for a cocktail, don't be afraid to improvise. There's nothing that fits the Pacific Island fantasy quite like sipping a cocktail out of a coconut. To open a coconut, first drain the water by hammering a nail into the 'eyes' and then draining the liquid (mix the coconut water with rum for a great drink). Hold the coconut on its side and chop into the shell using a large sharp knife (a machete is good if you have one), turning the coconut between chops. It will take a minute or two to cut through and be extremely careful of your fingers. Also, do this outside as bits of coconut shell can fly everywhere.

◄ Hollowed pineapple

Another great improvised drink container. Slice the top off the pineapple then run the knife in a circle around the inside of the skin. Cut across the core, then use a spoon to scoop out the flesh (save this for a pineapple daiquiri). I would also suggest slicing the bottom off the pineapple unless you don't intend on putting the drink down on a flat surface at any point.

GARNISHES

Once you've got your beautiful cocktail in an equally beautiful glass you need to jazz it up with a stunningly over-the-top garnish. Get really creative here. What would Carmen Miranda be without a buttload of fruit on her head?

There aren't really any rules when it comes to garnishes, but I like to choose something that contrasts nicely with the colour of the drink.

Wheel

I love a good wheel on a glass. So easy. Lie your citrus fruit of choice on its side and slice into rounds about 5 mm (¼ in) thick. Place into your drink or cut a slit into the middle and jam it on the side of your glass. BAM! Garnished.

Slice

This is your standard mixed drink garnish. Cut a citrus fruit in half lengthways and then slice into half circles. Easy.

Twist

A very classy garnish that also imparts flavour on your drink. With a sharp knife, carefully separate a strip of rind from your citrus fruit of choice, discarding any pith. Trim the edges and twist the strip over the drink so that the oil in the rind sprays into the glass. Rub the twist around the rim of the glass and drop into the drink.

Wedge

Another very easy way to garnish a glass. For smallish, roundish fruit (such as citrus), cut the fruit in half and cut into wedges. Add to your drink or make a small incision in the flesh and slide onto the rim of your glass. For larger fruit such as melon or pineapple, first cut into thick slices then cut the slices into wedges. Cut an incision, jam that baby onto the rim of your glass and party on.

Salt or sugar rim

This garnish also adds a flavour experience to the cocktail. Run the fleshy part of some fruit around the rim of your glass. Pour some sugar or salt onto a flat plate and carefully dunk the sticky rim into the granules. Drinks that have this kind of garnish should always be sipped without a straw.

Rum-Based Cocktails

Tiki is all about rum. White rum, dark rum, aged rum, demerara rum, French rum, Jamaican rum, Cuban rum, rum made from molasses, rum made from fresh sugar cane, over-proofed rum, navy rum, coconut rum, RUM RUM RUM!

Blending different kinds of rum together is where the true art of tiki cocktails comes into play. Any old hack bartender can mix rum and fruit juice, the real intricacies of a good tiki drink lies in the rum used to make it. Like any recipe worth it's salt, the better the ingredients you use, the better the drink will be. *Pas de la merde*, Monsieur Holmes.

Tiki is also all about fun with friends and entertaining. If you're working your way through the recipes in this book all by yourself, well, maybe you should be considering your life choices. Invite some friends over, tell them to wear grass skirts, coconut bras and bright, gaudy shirts. Also tell them to bring rum. If everyone brings a different bottle, your party is one step closer to success. You don't need all the rums in the shop, but you at least need a good white rum, a dark rum and a spiced rum.

DON THE BEACHCOMBER'S MAI TAI

IN THE LATE 30S AND EARLY 40S, THERE WAS A WAR GOING ON. I'M NOT TALKING ABOUT THE WAR IN EUROPE, I'M TALKING ABOUT THE MAI TAI WAR BETWEEN DON THE BEACHCOMBER AND TRADER VIC'S. BOTH CLAIMED TO HAVE INVENTED THE ICONIC DRINK. AND BOTH RECIPES ARE DIFFERENT.

THIS IS DONN BEACH'S RECIPE.

serves 1

60 ml (2 fl oz/¼ cup) aged rum
20 ml (¾ fl oz) orange curaçao
20 ml (¾ fl oz) Orgeat syrup
(page 252)

20 ml (¾ fl oz) freshly squeezed lime juice
mint sprig, for garnish

Combine the ingredients (except the garnish) in a cocktail shaker with ice. Shake.

Strain into an old fashioned glass filled with crushed ice. Garnish with mint.

TRADER VIC'S MAI TAI

... And this is Vic's. Rhum agricole is the French name for cane juice rum. Instead of being made from molasses, this rum is made from freshly squeezed sugar cane. It has a very different flavour to other rums.

serves 1

30 ml (1 fl oz) dark rum
30 ml (1 fl oz) rhum agricole
(cane juice rum)
3 teaspoons orange curaçao
1½ teaspoons Orgeat syrup
(page 252)

30 ml (1 fl oz) freshly squeezed
lime juice
mint sprig, for garnish

Combine the ingredients (except the garnish) in a cocktail shaker with ice. Shake.

Strain into an old fashioned glass filled with crushed ice. Garnish with mint.

QB COOLER

Some say that yes, Trader Vic invented the Mai Tai, but he based it on one of Don the Beachcomber's creations – the QB Cooler.

serves 1

30 ml (1 fl oz) gold rum

30 ml (1 fl oz) white rum

3 teaspoons demerara rum

2 teaspoons ginger liqueur

30 ml (1 fl oz) freshly squeezed orange juice

3 teaspoons freshly squeezed lime juice

3 teaspoons Honey syrup (page 253)

1½ teaspoons Velvet falernum (page 257)

30 ml (1 fl oz) soda water (seltzer)

2 dashes Orange bitters (page 258)

mint sprig, for garnish

Place the ingredients (except the garnish) in a high-speed blender with ½ cup crushed ice. Blend at high speed for 5 seconds.

Pour into a large old fashioned glass and top with crushed ice. Garnish with mint.

DRAGON 88 MAI TAI

A VARIATION ON THE CLASSIC, THIS COCKTAIL IS BASED ON ONE SERVED AT DRAGON 88 IN WEST BOYLSTON, MASSACHUSETTS. A MUCH MORE COMPLEX DRINK THAN ITS PREDECESSOR.

Serves 1

45 ml (1½ fl oz) rhum agricole (cane juice rum)

30 ml (1 fl oz) demerara rum

30 ml (1 fl oz) dark spiced rum

3 teaspoons orange curaçao

3 teaspoons freshly squeezed lime juice

3 teaspoons Orgeat syrup (page 252)

3 teaspoons Velvet falernum (page 257)

pineapple wedge and maraschino cherry, for garnish

Combine the ingredients (except the garnish) in a cocktail shaker with ice. Shake.

Strain into an old fashioned glass filled with crushed ice. Garnish with a pineapple wedge with a maraschino cherry and a straw.

BiTTER MAi TAi

For those times you want your Mai Tai before dinner – this is a delightfully boozy aperitif.

serves 1

30 ml (1 fl oz) dark rum
45 ml (1½ fl oz) Campari
3 teaspoons orange curaçao
30 ml (1 fl oz) freshly squeezed
   lime juice

20 ml (¾ fl oz) Orgeat syrup
   (page 252)
mint sprig, for garnish

Combine the ingredients (except the garnish) in a cocktail shaker filled with ice. Shake.

Strain into an old fashioned glass filled with crushed ice. Garnish with mint.

HURRICANE

THIS POTENT DRINK WAS DEVELOPED IN NEW ORLEANS IN THE 1940S AT A SPEAKEASY CALLED MR. O'BRIEN'S CLUB TIPPERARY (NOW TOURIST FAVOURITE PAT O'BRIEN'S BAR). DURING PROHIBITION THE PASSWORD TO GET IN WAS 'STORM'S BREWIN'. THE HURRICANE WAS INVENTED AS A WAY TO USE UP EXCESS RUM, BUT THE DRINK CAUGHT ON WITH THE SAILORS AND BECAME A MAINSTAY.

SERVES 1

60 ml (2 fl oz/¼ cup) white rum

60 ml (2 fl oz/¼ cup) dark rum

30 ml (1 fl oz) freshly squeezed lime juice

30 ml (1 fl oz) freshly squeezed orange juice

60 ml (2 fl oz/¼ cup) passionfruit pulp

3 teaspoons Passionfruit syrup (page 256)

3 teaspoons Sugar syrup (page 250)

3 teaspoons Grenadine (page 251)

1 teaspoon Orgeat syrup (page 252)

orange wheel and maraschino cherry, for garnish

Combine the ingredients (except the garnish) in a cocktail shaker with ice. Shake.

Strain into a hurricane glass filled with ice. Garnish with an orange wheel and maraschino cherry.

For an extra kick, finish the drink with over-proofed rum floated on top.

NAVY GROG

One of Donn Beach's originals. The name says it all.

Serves 1

30 ml (1 fl oz) dark rum
30 ml (1 fl oz) demerara rum
30 ml (1 fl oz) white rum
20 ml (¾ fl oz) freshly squeezed
 lime juice
20 ml (¾ fl oz) freshly squeezed
 grapefruit juice

30 ml (1 fl oz) Honey syrup
 (page 253)
30 ml (1 fl oz) soda water (seltzer)
lime wedge, for garnish

Combine the rums, fruit juices and honey syrup in a cocktail shaker filled with ice. Shake.

Strain into an old fashioned glass filled with crushed ice. Top with the soda water and garnish with a lime wedge.

Traditionally this drink is garnished with a frozen 'snow cone' with a straw through the middle. You can make your own by filling a cone-shaped glass with finely crushed ice, poking a straw through the centre and freezing it for a few hours.

COLONIAL GROG

A VARIATION OF DONN BEACH'S CLASSIC DRINK; THIS COCKTAIL WAS CREATED BY TIKI HISTORIAN JEFF 'BEACHBUM' BERRY.

serves 1

3 teaspoons dark rum

3 teaspoons gold rum

3 teaspoons freshly squeezed lime juice

3 teaspoons freshly squeezed orange juice

3 teaspoons soda water (seltzer)

2 teaspoons maple syrup

1 teaspoon Allspice dram (page 259)

1 dash Orange bitters (page 258)

orange wheel, for garnish

Place the ingredients (except the garnish) in a high-speed blender with ½ cup crushed ice. Blend at high speed for 5 seconds.

Strain into an old fashioned glass filled with crushed ice. Garnish with an orange wheel.

Traditionally, this drink is served in a glass lined with a shell of crushed ice. To do this, fill an old fashioned glass with finely crushed ice. With a spoon, slowly create a well in the middle, pushing the ice up the side of the glass. When you have a well in the ice, put the glass in the freezer for a few hours before serving.

COFFEE GROG

MAYBE YOU'RE LOOKING FOR A BREAKFAST GROG? OR GROG TO WARM YOU ON A COLD NIGHT ON THE HIGH SEAS? THIS RUM TODDY WILL SURELY GET THE SHIVER OUT OF YOUR TIMBERS.

serves 1

½ teaspoon sugar
1 teaspoon Coffee grog batter (page 261)
1 pinch ground nutmeg
1 pinch ground clove
1 pinch ground cinnamon
3 strips orange rind

1 strip grapefruit rind
180 ml (6 fl oz) freshly brewed coffee
3 teaspoons aged rum
3 teaspoons 151 proof dark rum
cinnamon stick, for garnish

Place the sugar, batter, spices and rind in a large warmed mug or heatproof glass. Pour in the hot coffee and stir until the sugar is dissolved.

Combine the rums in a metal ladle or small heatproof jug and carefully ignite. Pour the flaming rum into the coffee mixture and garnish with a cinnamon stick.

PLANTER'S PUNCH

A wine-glass with lemon juice fill,
Of sugar the same glass fill twice
Then rub them together until
The mixture looks smooth, soft, and nice.

Of rum then three wine glasses add,
And four of cold water please take. A
Drink then you'll have that's not bad
At least, so they say in Jamaica.

– Fun Magazine, September, 1878

Planter's punch pre-dates tiki, but it fits the bill nicely.
Also available in party size on page 230.

serves 1

45 ml (1½ fl oz) dark rum
30 ml (1 fl oz) white rum
30 ml (1 fl oz) freshly squeezed
   lemon juice
30 ml (1 fl oz) Honey syrup
   (page 253)

2 dashes Orange bitters (page 258)
60 ml (2 fl oz/¼ cup) soda water
   (seltzer)
mint spring, pineapple wedge and
   maraschino cherry, for garnish

Combine the rums, lemon juice, honey syrup and bitters in a cocktail
shaker filled with ice. Shake.

Strain into a large glass filled with ice cubes. Top with the soda and
garnish with mint, a pineapple wedge and maraschino cherry.

Tiki SwiZZLE

Swizzle sticks can turn the mundane into a fun day. Used for stirring or skewering garnishes, swizzle sticks were originally made out of wood, with the tops carved into tiki heads to really decorate your drink.

serves 1

45 ml (1½ fl oz) spiced rum
20 ml (¾ fl oz) dark rum
3 teaspoons freshly squeezed
lime juice
3 teaspoons Passionfruit syrup
(page 256)

3 teaspoons Sugar syrup
(page 250)
2 dashes Orange bitters (page 258)
passionfruit pulp and pineapple
wedge, for garnish

Place the ingredients (except the garnish) in a high-speed blender with 1 cup crushed ice. Blend at high speed for 5 seconds.

Pour into a chilled swizzle or other stainless steel cup and top with crushed ice. Garnish with passionfruit pulp and a pineapple wedge.

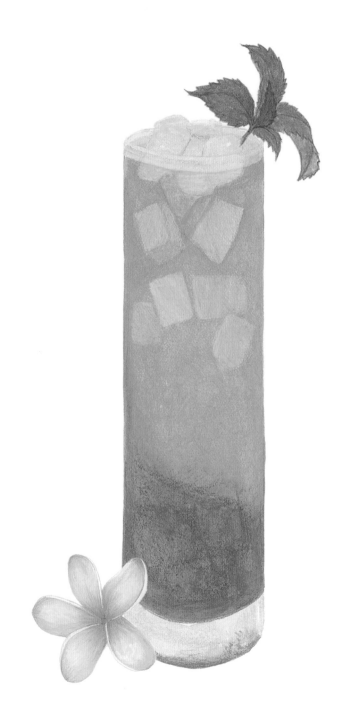

ZOMBiE

ANOTHER DONN BEACH ORIGINAL, NAMED FOR THE STATE YOU'RE LIKELY TO FIND YOURSELF IN AFTER DRINKING THREE OF THESE LETHAL CONCOCTIONS.

serves 1

45 ml (1½ fl oz) gold rum
45 ml (1½ fl oz) dark rum
30 ml (1 fl oz) 151 proof demerara rum
20 ml (¾ fl oz) freshly squeezed lime juice
3 teaspoons Velvet falernum (page 257)

1 teaspoon Grenadine (page 251)
1 teaspoon Pernod
1 dash Orange bitters (page 258)
3 teaspoons Don's mix (page 261)
mint sprig, for garnish

Place the ingredients (except the garnish) in a high-speed blender with ¾ cup crushed ice. Blend at high speed for 5 seconds.

Pour into a tall glass and top up with ice cubes. Garnish with mint and drink responsibly.

CLASSIC DAIQUIRI

One of the simplest cocktails, yet one of the best. Rum, sugar and lime are long-time lovers. They deserve to be together.

serves 1

60 ml (2 fl oz/¼ cup) white rum
30 ml (1 fl oz) freshly squeezed
    lime juice

3 teaspoons Sugar syrup
    (page 250)
lime wheel, for garnish

Combine the ingredients (except the garnish) in a cocktail shaker filled with ice. Shake.

Strain into a chilled cocktail glass and garnish with a lime wheel.

PINEAPPLE DAIQUIRI

Just like a regular Daiquiri, only this one makes use of the best of the tropical fruits (in my humble opinion).

serves 1

80 g (2¾ oz/½ cup) chopped fresh pineapple
5 mint leaves
60 ml (2 fl oz/¼ cup) pineapple rum
30 ml (1 fl oz) freshly squeezed lime juice

3 teaspoons Sugar syrup (page 250)
pineapple wedge, for garnish

Muddle the pineapple and mint in a cocktail shaker. Add the rum, lime and sugar syrup and fill the shaker with ice. Shake vigorously.

Strain into a chilled cocktail glass. Garnish with a pineapple wedge.

FROZEN LIME DAIQUIRI

THIS GROWN-UP SLUSHY IS THE PERFECT START FOR SO MANY GOOD TIMES IN THE SUNSHINE.

SERVES 1

90 ml (3 fl oz) white rum
60 ml (2 fl oz/¼ cup) freshly
 squeezed lime juice

30 ml (1 fl oz) Sugar syrup
 (page 250)
lime wheel, for garnish

Place the ingredients (except the garnish) in a high-speed blender with 1 cup ice. Blend at high speed until smooth.

Pour into a large cocktail glass and garnish with a lime wheel.

MANGO DAIQUIRI

WHEN MANGOES ARE IN SEASON, IT'S TIME FOR MANGO DAIQUIRIS. THE TEXTURE OF THIS DRINK IS LIKE SIPPING VELVET THROUGH SILK SHEETS. THIS DRINK ALSO WORKS REALLY WELL WITH TINNED MANGOES, JUST USE LESS SUGAR SYRUP.

serves 1

60 ml (2 fl oz/¼ cup) white rum
20 ml (¾ fl oz) mango liqueur
  (optional)
30 ml (1 fl oz) freshly squeezed
  lime juice

1 mango, cheeks removed and
  stone discarded
20 ml (¾ fl oz) Sugar syrup
  (page 250)
lime wheel, for garnish

Scoop the flesh from the mango cheeks and place in a high-speed blender with the rest of the ingredients (except the garnish) and ½ cup crushed ice. Blend at high speed until smooth.

Pour into a large cocktail glass and garnish with a lime wedge.

STRAWBERRY DAIQUIRI

The key to a really good strawberry daiquiri is lots and lots of good-quality strawberries. You'd be surprised at how much booze you can hide in one of these babies.

Serves 1

250 g (9 oz) fresh strawberries, hulled and cut in half

55 g (2 oz/¼ cup) sugar

30 ml (1 fl oz) freshly squeezed lemon juice

60 ml (2 fl oz/¼ cup) white rum

20 ml (¾ fl oz) strawberry liqueur (optional)

20 ml (¾ fl oz) freshly squeezed lime juice

20 ml (¾ fl oz) Sugar syrup (page 250)

lime wheel and strawberries, for garnish

In a small bowl, combine the strawberries with the sugar and lemon juice. Cover and refrigerate for 30 minutes.

Place the strawberries in a high-speed blender with the rest of the ingredients (except the garnish) and 1 cup ice. Blend at high speed until smooth.

Pour into a large cocktail glass and garnish with a lime wheel and sliced strawberries.

BAHAMA MAMA

Just like my mama, this one is quite alcoholic. A delightful balance of rums and fruit juice that gets stronger as you get closer to the bottom, thanks to the 151 float.

Serves 1

30 ml (1 fl oz) dark rum
3 teaspoons white rum
3 teaspoons coconut rum
90 ml (3 fl oz) pineapple juice, fresh if possible
60 ml (2 fl oz/¼ cup) freshly squeezed orange juice

30 ml (1 fl oz) freshly squeezed lemon juice
1 dash Orange bitters (page 258)
1 teaspoon Grenadine (page 251)
3 teaspoons 151 proof rum
pineapple wedge, orange wheel and maraschino cherry, for garnish

Combine the dark, white and coconut rums with the fruit juices and bitters in a cocktail shaker filled with ice. Shake.

Strain into a poco grande or other tall glass filled with ice.

Add the grenadine, pouring it slowly against the inside of the glass (it should sink to the bottom). Float the 151 proof rum on top by pouring it over the back of a spoon.

Garnish with a pineapple wedge, orange wheel and maraschino cherry, and drink through a straw.

Tiki-Ti Five-0

This drink was originally created by tiki historian Jeff 'Beachbum' Berry for a celebration of 50 years of tiki cocktails. The use of ginger and five-spice is a nod to the exotic spices used in the early days of tiki.

Serves 1

60 ml (2 fl oz/¼ cup) aged rum

30 ml (1 fl oz) Honey syrup (page 253)

30 ml (1 fl oz) freshly squeezed lime juice

3 teaspoons freshly squeezed orange juice

2 teaspoons ginger liqueur

1 pinch Chinese five-spice, plus extra for garnish

lime slice and candied ginger, for garnish

Combine the ingredients (except the garnish) in a cocktail shaker filled with ice. Shake.

Pour the contents of the shaker into a tall glass. Garnish with five-spice, a lime slice and candied ginger.

PAINKILLER

This cocktail was created by Pusser's Rum, a company that makes a blended rum from the original Royal Navy recipe. It's a potent rum, at a whopping 54% ABV. The company was founded after the navy stopped giving out a daily rum ration.

Serves 1

60–90 ml (2–3 fl oz) aged rum

125 ml (4 fl oz/½ cup) pineapple juice, fresh if possible

30 ml (1 fl oz) freshly squeezed orange juice

3 teaspoons coconut cream

3 teaspoons Sugar syrup (page 250)

pineapple wedge, maraschino cherry and freshly grated nutmeg, for garnish

Combine the ingredients (except the garnish) in a cocktail shaker filled with ice. Shake.

Strain into an old fashioned glass filled with crushed ice. Garnish with a pineapple wedge and freshly grated nutmeg.

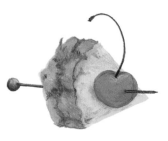

THE ANCIENT MARINER

One of Jeff 'Beachbum' Berry's cocktails, created when he was attempting to unlock the secrets of Donn Beach's Navy Grog. He named it the Ancient Mariner because that's how old he felt after he'd finished.

serves 1

30 ml (1 fl oz) demerara rum
30 ml (1 fl oz) dark rum
20 ml (¾ fl oz) freshly squeezed
  lime juice
3 teaspoons freshly squeezed
  grapefruit juice

3 teaspoons Sugar syrup
  (page 250)
1½ teaspoons Allspice dram
  (page 259)
mint sprig and lime wedge,
  for garnish

Combine the ingredients (except the garnish) in a cocktail shaker filled with ice. Shake.

Pour the contents of the shaker into a tiki mug or old fashioned glass and top up with more ice if necessary.

Garnish with mint and a lime wedge.

41

BEACHCOMBER

A VARIATION ON DONN BEACH'S DAIQUIRI.

Serves 1

60 ml (2 fl oz/¼ cup) white rum
20 ml (¾ fl oz) orange curaçao
20 ml (¾ fl oz) freshly squeezed lime juice
1½ teaspoons maraschino cherry liqueur (or juice)

¼ teaspoon Sugar syrup (page 250)
orange wheel and maraschino cherry, for garnish

Combine the ingredients (except the garnish) in a cocktail shaker filled with ice. Shake.

Strain into a chilled martini glass and garnish with an orange wheel and a maraschino cherry.

PAMPANITO

Another modern tiki recipe, this one comes from a bar called Smuggler's Cove in San Francisco. The cocktail is named after Pampero Especial, a dark, blended rum from Venezuela that is aged in oak.

serves 1

45 ml (1½ fl oz) aged rum
30 ml (1 fl oz) freshly squeezed
  lemon juice
3 teaspoons light molasses
3 teaspoons Sugar syrup
  (page 250)

1½ teaspoons Allspice dram
  (page 259)
1 dash Orange bitters (page 258)
90 ml (3 fl oz) soda water (seltzer)
lemon twist, for garnish

Combine the rum, lemon juice, molasses, sugar syrup, allspice dram and bitters in a cocktail shaker filled with ice. Shake.

Strain into a tall glass filled with ice, top with the soda water and stir. Garnish with a lemon twist.

WICKED WAHINE

Brice Ginardi created this drink after he moved to Hawaii and was dismayed to find the tiki craze hadn't taken off over there. So what did he do? He opened his own bar and made this wicked whistle whetter.

serves 1

45 ml (1½ fl oz) spiced rum
1½ teaspoons Velvet falernum
(page 257)
1½ teaspoons freshly squeezed
lemon juice
1½ teaspoons freshly squeezed
lime juice

1½ teaspoons Passionfruit syrup
(page 256)
1½ teaspoons Grenadine
(page 251)
1 dash Orange bitters (page 258)
edible flower, for garnish

Combine the ingredients (except the garnish) in a cocktail shaker filled with ice. Shake.

Strain into a chilled cocktail glass and garnish with an edible flower.

TANGAROA

ANOTHER ONE OF BEACHBUM BERRY'S. HE WAS NEVER TAKEN BY THE FLAVOUR OF MANGO IN HIS DRINKS UNTIL HE ADDED SOME NUTS. AMARETTO IS AN ALMOND LIQUEUR THAT REALLY COMPLEMENTS THE FLAVOUR OF MANGO.

SERVES 1

30 ml (1 fl oz) white rum
30 ml (1 fl oz) gold rum
1½ teaspoons amaretto
60 ml (2 fl oz/¼ cup) mango nectar

3 teaspoons freshly squeezed lime juice
cinnamon stick, for garnish

Combine the ingredients (except the garnish) in a cocktail shaker filled with ice. Shake.

Strain into a chilled champagne flute and garnish with a cinnamon stick.

NEVER SAY DIE

Words to live by. This one comes from Don the Beachcomber, but later in the piece – circa 1960s. Perhaps Beach was foreseeing the end of the tiki era.

Serves 1

30 ml (1 fl oz) aged rum
3 teaspoons white rum
3 teaspoons dark rum
3 teaspoons freshly squeezed lime juice
3 teaspoons freshly squeezed orange juice

3 teaspoons pineapple juice, fresh if possible
3 teaspoons Honey syrup (page 253)
1 dash Orange bitters (page 258)
pink grapefruit slice, for garnish

Place the ingredients (except the garnish) in a high-speed blender with ½ cup crushed ice. Blend at high speed for 5 seconds.

Pour into an old fashioned glass and top with crushed ice.

Garnish with a pink grapefruit slice.

POLYNESIAN PEARL DIVER

THIS DONN BEACH CLASSIC USES BUTTER IN THE PEARL DIVER'S MIX (NOT A COMMON INGREDIENT TO REACH FOR WHEN MAKING COCKTAILS). THE PEARL DIVER HAS ITS OWN SPECIFIC GLASS, BUT A COCONUT WILL ALSO DO THE TRICK.

serves 1

45 ml (1½ fl oz) white rum
3 teaspoons demerara rum
3 teaspoons dark rum
1 tablespoon Velvet falernum (page 257)
30 ml (1 fl oz) freshly squeezed orange juice

20 ml (¾ fl oz) Pearl diver's mix (page 260)
Pearl diver glass or opened coconut, for serving (optional)
edible flower, for garnish

Place the ingredients (except the garnish) in a high-speed blender with 1 cup crushed ice. Blend at high speed until smooth.

Pour into a Pearl diver glass or coconut and garnish with an edible flower.

ViCiOUS ViRGiN #1

THIS LITTLE BEAUTY IS NOT AS INNOCENT AS SHE LOOKS AND YOU WILL NEED TO TREAT HER WITH THE RESPECT SHE DESERVES. POP A CHERRY INTO THIS ONE TO GARNISH.

serves 1

3 teaspoons dark rum
30 ml (1 fl oz) white rum
1½ teaspoons Velvet falernum
  (page 257)

3 teaspoons orange curaçao
20 ml (¾ fl oz) freshly squeezed
  lime juice
maraschino cherry, for garnish

Place the ingredients (except the garnish) in a high-speed blender with ½ cup ice and blend until smooth.

Pour into a chilled champagne flute. Garnish with a maraschino cherry.

VICIOUS VIRGIN #2

The more colourful sister of the family. This girl likes to party but she ain't givin' it up easily.

serves 1

20 ml (¾ fl oz) white rum
20 ml (¾ fl oz) silver tequila
1 teaspoon blue curaçao
3 teaspoons Orgeat syrup
  (page 252)

20 ml (¾ fl oz) freshly squeezed
  lime juice
45 ml (1½ fl oz) freshly squeezed
  grapefruit juice
maraschino cherry, for garnish

Combine the ingredients (except the garnish) in a cocktail shaker filled with ice. Shake.

Strain into a chilled cocktail glass. Garnish with a maraschino cherry.

DEMERARA DRY FLOAT

Demerara rum comes from Guyana in northern South America.
It is aged in oak barrels, but unlike other aged rums, the humidity
in Guyana seems to age the rum faster. This drink can definitely
be doubled if you want more of a kick.

Serves 1

30 ml (1 fl oz) demerara rum
30 ml (1 fl oz) freshly squeezed lime
  juice
1½ teaspoons freshly squeezed
  lemon juice
3 teaspoons Passionfruit syrup
  (page 256)

1½ teaspoons maraschino cherry
  liqueur (or juice)
3 teaspoons 151 proof
  demerara rum
maraschino cherry, for garnish

Combine the demerara rum, fruit juices, passionfruit syrup and cherry
liqueur in a cocktail shaker filled with ice. Shake.

Strain into a large old fashioned glass filled with crushed ice. Carefully
float the 151 proof rum on top by pouring it over the back of a spoon.

Garnish with a maraschino cherry and drink through a straw.

QUEEN'S ROAD COCKTAIL

Ginger liqueur is one of my favourite cocktail ingredients. It adds a spiciness and heat to the drink that I can't get enough of. This drink is perfectly balanced and you will definitely have more than one.

serves 1

45 ml (1½ fl oz) gold rum
1 teaspoon ginger liqueur
3 teaspoons freshly squeezed
   lime juice
3 teaspoons freshly squeezed
   orange juice

3 teaspoons Honey syrup
   (page 253)
1 dash Orange bitters (page 258)
orange twist, for garnish

Combine the ingredients (except the garnish) in a cocktail shaker filled with ice. Shake.

Strain into a chilled cocktail glass. Garnish with an orange twist.

PIÑA COLADA

Do you like Piña Coladas? And getting caught in the rain? This is possibly the most famous tropical resort drink of all. Pineapple, coconut and loads of fruit to garnish. This drink should end up looking like Carmen Miranda's hat.

Serves 1

30 ml (1 fl oz) gold rum
30 ml (1 fl oz) white rum
50 ml (1¾ fl oz) coconut milk
40 ml (1¼ fl oz) Sugar syrup
  (page 250)
80 ml (2½ fl oz/⅓ cup) pineapple
  juice, fresh if possible

20 ml (¾ fl oz) freshly squeezed
  lime juice
3 teaspoons thick (double/heavy)
  cream
pineapple wedge, maraschino
  cherry and cocktail umbrella,
  for garnish

Place the ingredients (except the garnish) in a high-speed blender with 1 cup ice. Pulse until the ice is crushed.

Pour into a poco grande or other tall glass and garnish with a pineapple wedge, maraschino cherry and cocktail umbrella.

CUBA LiBRE

This drink is said to have come about during the Spanish–American war, circa 1902. The name literally means 'Free Cuba'. To honour this, you should definitely use Cuban rum and drink while smoking a cigar.

serves 1

45 ml (1½ fl oz) dark Cuban rum
30 ml (1 fl oz) freshly squeezed
    lime juice

60 ml (2 fl oz/¼ cup) cola
lime wedge (and a Cuban cigar),
    for garnish

Combine the ingredients (except the garnish) in a tall glass filled with crushed ice and stir to combine.

Garnish with a lime wedge and smoke the cigar.

TAHITIAN BREEZE

BEST ENJOYED WHILE WEARING A GRASS SKIRT AND DIPPING YOUR TOES IN THE WATER.

SERVES 1

30 ml (1 fl oz) white rum

30 ml (1 fl oz) gold rum

30 ml (1 fl oz) freshly squeezed pink grapefruit juice

30 ml (1 fl oz) freshly squeezed orange juice

3 teaspoons Passionfruit syrup (page 256)

passionfruit pulp and pink grapefruit wheel, for garnish

Place the ingredients (except the garnish) in a high-speed blender with crushed ice. Blend at high speed for 5 seconds.

Pour into a tall glass. Float the passionfruit pulp on top and garnish with a grapefruit wheel.

ROYAL CANADIAN KILTED YAKSMAN

MAPLE SYRUP ADDS A LOVELY COMPLEXITY TO DRINKS. IT GOES ESPECIALLY WELL WITH SPICED RUM AND CAN BE USED IN PLACE OF SUGAR SYRUP.

Serves 1

30 ml (1 fl oz) spiced rum
30 ml (1 fl oz) dark rum
2 teaspoons Cinnamon syrup
  (page 255)
2 teaspoons maple syrup

30 ml (1 fl oz) freshly squeezed
  lime juice
60 ml (2 fl oz/¼ cup) ginger beer
cinnamon stick, for garnish

Place the rums, syrups and lime juice in a high-speed blender with 1 cup crushed ice and blend at high speed for 5 seconds.

Pour into a highball glass and top with more crushed ice. Top with the ginger beer.

Garnish with a cinnamon stick.

FEDERALi

AGAVE SYRUP COMES FROM THE AGAVE PLANT; THE SAME PLANT WE GET TEQUILA FROM. IT HAS A GREAT EARTHY FLAVOUR THAT WORKS SO WELL IN COCKTAILS.

serves 1

30 ml (1 fl oz) white rum
30 ml (1 fl oz) aged rum
2 teaspoons agave syrup
2 teaspoons Orgeat syrup
   (page 252)

30 ml (1 fl oz) freshly squeezed
   lemon juice
orange wheel, for garnish

Combine the ingredients (except the garnish) in a cocktail shaker filled with ice. Shake.

Strain into an old fashioned glass filled with crushed ice. Garnish with an orange wheel.

NUI NUI

THIS WAS ONE OF THE RECIPES DONN BEACH KEPT CLOSE TO HIS CHEST.
IT TOOK JEFF 'BEACHBUM' BERRY MANY YEARS TO TRACK DOWN THE
SECRET INGREDIENTS IN BEACH'S SYRUPS AND BITTERS. A VERY SPECIAL
COCKTAIL INDEED.

Serves 1

60 ml (2 fl oz/¼ cup) gold rum

3 teaspoons freshly squeezed lime juice

3 teaspoons freshly squeezed orange juice

1½ teaspoons Cinnamon syrup (page 255)

1 teaspoon Allspice dram (page 259)

1 teaspoon Vanilla syrup (page 254)

1 dash Orange bitters (page 258)

orange twist, for garnish

Place the ingredients (except the garnish) in a high-speed blender with 1 cup crushed ice. Blend at high speed for 5 seconds.

Pour into a tiki mug and top with crushed ice. Garnish with an orange twisted straw.

DARK AND STORMY

A CLASSIC WAY TO DRINK RUM. SIMPLE, TALL AND WITH A TOUCH OF
BITTERNESS. JUST LIKE ME.

serves 1

45 ml (1½ fl oz) dark rum
30 ml (1 fl oz) freshly squeezed
   lime juice
2 dashes Orange bitters (page 258)

60 ml (2 fl oz/¼ cup) ginger beer
lime wedge, for garnish

Combine the ingredients (except the garnish) in a tall glass filled with
crushed ice and stir to combine.

Garnish with a lime wedge.

ViEQUENSE

Isla de Vieques is an island off Puerto Rico. It's unclear as to whether the drink originated from the island, or if the maker was just creating a tribute to the place and its people – either way, it's like the essence of the Caribbean in a glass.

serves 1

60 ml (2 fl oz/¼ cup) dark rum
30 ml (1 fl oz) amaretto
60 ml (2 fl oz/¼ cup) freshly squeezed orange juice

60 ml (2 fl oz/¼ cup) coconut cream
orange slice and maraschino cherry, for garnish

Combine the ingredients (except the garnish) in a cocktail shaker filled with ice. Shake.

Strain into a tall glass filled with ice. Garnish with an orange slice and a maraschino cherry.

ORANGE WHIP

1980s Chicago is hardly what you'd associate with the tropical vibes of tiki, but John Candy made this drink big again after mentioning it in an improvised scene in The *Blues Brothers* – turns out, he was actually plugging a brand of orange soda. No matter, we can still imagine the big guy sipping on one of these.

Serves 1

30 ml (1 fl oz) white rum
30 ml (1 fl oz) dark rum
3 teaspoons orange curaçao
30 ml (1 fl oz) freshly squeezed lime juice

45 ml (1½ fl oz) freshly squeezed orange juice
1 teaspoon Grenadine (page 251)
orange wheel, for garnish

Place the ingredients (except the garnish) in a high-speed blender with 1 cup ice and blend at high speed until smooth.

Pour into a cocktail glass. Garnish with an orange wheel.

JAMAICAN FLOAT

WHAT MAKES A JAMAICAN FLOAT? PROBABLY A HIGHER DENSITY OF SALT IN THE WATER.

Serves 1

60 ml (2 fl oz/¼ cup) white rum
45 ml (1½ fl oz) freshly squeezed orange juice
3 teaspoons freshly squeezed lemon juice

2 teaspoons Orgeat syrup (page 252)
1 teaspoon Grenadine (page 251)
30 ml (1 fl oz) Jamaican rum
orange wheel, for garnish

Combine the white rum, fruit juices and orgeat syrup in a cocktail shaker filled with ice. Shake.

Strain into a tall glass filled with ice. Add the grenadine and float the Jamaican rum on top by pouring it over the back of a spoon.

Garnish with an orange wheel and drink through a straw.

CRADLE OF LiFE

THIS ONE HAS FIRE ON IT! THE LIME GETS TURNED INSIDE OUT, FILLED WITH
CHARTREUSE AND SET ALIGHT. THIS NOT ONLY LOOKS AWESOME, BUT IT
ALSO RELEASES THE OILS IN THE SKIN OF THE LIME, REALLY ADDING TO THE
COMPLEXITY OF THIS DRINK.

serves 1

30 ml (1 fl oz) aged rum
30 ml (1 fl oz) spiced rum
3 teaspoons freshly squeezed
lemon juice
3 teaspoons freshly squeezed lime
juice (reserve 1 squeezed lime
half for garnish)
3 teaspoons freshly squeezed
orange juice

3 teaspoons Orgeat syrup
(page 252)
½ teaspoon Orange bitters
(page 258)
½ lime
2 teaspoons green chartreuse

Combine the rums, fruit juices, syrup and bitters in a cocktail shaker
(no ice). Shake.

Strain into an old fashioned glass filled with crushed ice.

Place the reserved lime half in the top of the drink.

Fill the lime cup with green chartreuse and carefully ignite. After
15 seconds, blow out the flame and tip the chartreuse into the drink.

THE FLAMING WISDOM OF PELÉ

This is a take on the creation of tiki bartender Blaire Reynolds from Portland, Oregon. It uses all the classic tiki flavours and packs one hell of a rum punch. Don't spend the whole night on these.

serves 1

30 ml (1 fl oz) 151 proof rum, plus extra for garnish

30 ml (1 fl oz) dark rum

30 ml (1 fl oz) white rum

3 teaspoons aged rum

20 ml (¾ fl oz) freshly squeezed lime juice (reserve 1 squeezed lime half for garnish)

20 ml (¾ fl oz) freshly squeezed grapefruit juice

20 ml (¾ fl oz) Velvet falernum (page 257)

3 teaspoons Honey syrup (page 253)

1½ teaspoons Cinnamon syrup (page 255)

2 dashes Orange bitters (page 258)

Combine the ingredients (except the reserved lime half) in a cocktail shaker filled with ice. Shake.

Strain into a tiki mug or tall glass filled with crushed ice.

Invert the reserved lime half so that the skin side creates a cup. Place in the top of the drink.

Fill the lime cup with extra 151 proof rum and carefully ignite. After 15 seconds, blow out the flame and tip the rum into the drink.

TEST PiLOT

THIS ONE GOES ALL THE WAY BACK TO 1941 FROM THE COCKTAIL LIST AT DON THE BEACHCOMBER. THERE WAS A 'SECRET INGREDIENT' IN THIS DRINK THAT TURNED OUT TO BE A COMBINATION OF PERNOD AND ANGOSTURA BITTERS. NEITHER FLAVOUR SHOULD BE FLYING THE PLANE IN THIS DRINK BUT THEY SHOULD BE SOMEWHERE IN THE COCKPIT.

serves 1

45 ml (1½ fl oz) dark rum
20 ml (¾ fl oz) white rum
2 teaspoons orange curaçao
1 teaspoon Pernod
3 teaspoons freshly squeezed
lime juice

3 teaspoons Velvet falernum
(page 257)
1 dash Orange bitters (page 258)
orange wheel, for garnish

Place the ingredients (except the garnish) in a high-speed blender with 1 cup ice. Blend at high speed until smooth.

Pour into a large cocktail glass and garnish with an orange wheel.

JET PiLOT

Once the Test Pilot graduated from flight school, she became a Jet Pilot. She's a sassy little number. As long as you treat her with respect, she won't hurt you in the morning.

Serves 1

30 ml (1 fl oz) dark rum
20 ml (¾ fl oz) white rum
20 ml (¾ fl oz) 151 proof demerara rum
1 teaspoon Pernod
3 teaspoons freshly squeezed grapefruit juice

3 teaspoons freshly squeezed lime juice
3 teaspoons Cinnamon syrup (page 255)
1 dash Orange bitters (page 258)
maraschino cherry, for garnish

Place the ingredients (except the garnish) in a high-speed blender with 1 cup ice. Blend at high speed until smooth.

Pour into a large cocktail glass and garnish with a maraschino cherry.

THE NIGHT MARCHER

This is a signature cocktail from Tar Pit, a restaurant and bar in LA. A modern take on the tiki style with a solid hit of rum and a good kick of hot sauce.

Serves 1

80 ml (2½ fl oz/⅓ cup) aged rum

3 teaspoons 151 proof rum

3 teaspoons green chartreuse

20 ml (¾ fl oz) freshly squeezed lime juice

20 ml (¾ fl oz) Demerara sugar syrup (page 250)

1 dash hot sauce

2 dashes Orange bitters (page 258)

60 ml (2 fl oz/¼ cup) ginger beer

lime wedge and candied ginger, for garnish

Place the liquor, lime juice, sugar syrup, hot sauce and bitters in a tall glass. Stir well to combine.

Fill the glass with crushed ice and top with the ginger beer. Garnish with a lime wedge and candied ginger.

COCONUT RUM

Coconut rum, by itself, is not the greatest drink in the world. But mix it up with a bunch of other stuff and chuck it in a coconut? That's a whole 'nother story.

Serves 1

30 ml (1 fl oz) white rum
30 ml (1 fl oz) dark rum
3 teaspoons coconut rum
30 ml (1 fl oz) freshly squeezed lime juice
1 handful mint leaves, chopped
60 ml (2 fl oz/¼ cup) coconut water
3 teaspoons Orgeat syrup (page 252)

3 teaspoons Sugar syrup (page 250)
opened coconut, for serving (optional)
90 ml (3 fl oz) ginger beer
pineapple wedge and cocktail umbrella, for garnish

Combine the rums, lime juice, mint, coconut water and syrups in a cocktail shaker filled with ice. Shake.

Strain into a coconut (or a large cocktail glass) filled with crushed ice and top with the ginger beer.

Garnish with a pineapple wedge and cocktail umbrella.

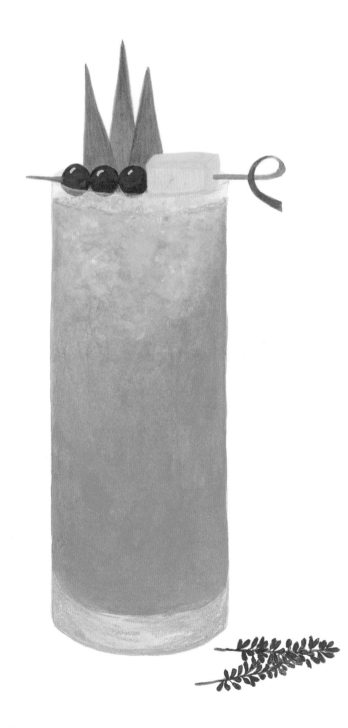

THREE DOTS AND A DASH

THREE DOTS AND A DASH IS 'V' IN MORSE CODE, USED AT THE END OF THE WAR TO COMMUNICATE VICTORY. DONN BEACH CREATED THIS DRINK TO CELEBRATE THE RETURN OF THE TROOPS, THE VICTORY CODE SPELLED OUT IN THE GARNISH USING CHERRIES AND PINEAPPLE.

serves 1

1 pineapple stick, for garnish
3 maraschino cherries, for garnish
30 ml (1 fl oz) rhum agricole
  (cane juice rum)
30 ml (1 fl oz) aged rum
30 ml (1 fl oz) lime juice
3 teaspoons orange curaçao

3 teaspoons Honey syrup
  (page 253)
3 teaspoons Velvet falernum
  (page 257)
1½ teaspoons Allspice dram
  (page 259)
3 dashes Orange bitters (page 258)

To make the garnish, thread the pineapple stick and three cherries onto a skewer.

Place the ingredients (except the garnish) in a high-speed blender with ½ cup crushed ice. Blend at high speed for 5 seconds.

Pour into a tall glass and top with crushed ice. Place the skewer across the top, ensuring that it's facing the right way so it reads as three dots and a dash.

RUM JULEP

Donn Beach's take on the classic Kentucky Derby cocktail. Although there is no mint in this drink, the allspice dram and falernum add a nice herbal quality. Giddy up.

serves 1

45 ml (1½ fl oz) demerara rum
3 teaspoons aged rum
3 teaspoons freshly squeezed lime juice
3 teaspoons freshly squeezed orange juice
3 teaspoons Honey syrup (page 253)

¼ teaspoon Grenadine (page 251)
¼ teaspoon Velvet falernum (page 257)
¼ teaspoon Allspice dram (page 259)
1 dash Orange bitters (page 258)

Place the ingredients (except the garnish) in a high-speed blender with ½ cup crushed ice. Blend at high speed for 5 seconds.

Pour into a metal julep cup or tall glass and top with crushed ice.

MYSTERY GARDENIA

One of Don the Beachcomber's from the mid 60s. Beach didn't mind using butter in his cocktails to give a richness and texture like nothing else. This is a drink that will drape itself around your neck and say, 'Aloha.'

serves 1

2 teaspoons honey, warmed
2 teaspoons unsalted butter, softened
45 ml (1½ fl oz) white rum

3 teaspoons freshly squeezed lime juice
1 dash Orange bitters (page 258)
mint sprig, for garnish

In a small bowl, whip the honey and butter together.

Combine with the rest of the ingredients (except the garnish) in a high-speed blender with ½ cup crushed ice. Blend at high speed for 5 seconds.

Pour into a chilled cocktail glass. Garnish with mint.

Pi Yi

ONE THING THAT WILL REALLY SELL A COCKTAIL IS SERVING IT IN A RIDICULOUS VESSEL. IF YOU'RE SITTING BY THE POOL, UNDER A BLUE SKY AND GENTLY WAVING PALM TREES, AND A WAITER DELIVERS YOU A COCKTAIL SERVED IN A HOLLOWED-OUT PINEAPPLE, YOU CAN GUARANTEE THAT EVERYONE ELSE WILL WANT ONE.

Serves 1

30 ml (1 fl oz) white rum

30 ml (1 fl oz) gold rum

45 ml (1½ fl oz) pineapple juice, fresh if possible

3 teaspoons Honey syrup (page 253)

3 teaspoons Passionfruit syrup (page 256)

1 dash Orange bitters (page 258)

hollowed pineapple, for serving (optional)

pineapple leaves and maraschino cherries, for garnish

Place the rums, pineapple juice, syrups and bitters in a high-speed blender with ½ cup crushed ice. Blend at high speed for 5 seconds.

Pour into a hollowed-out pineapple (or large cocktail glass) and top with crushed ice.

Garnish with pineapple leaves and maraschino cherries.

MISSiONARY'S DOWNFALL

This is one of Donn Beach's oldest creations, appearing at his bar somewhere around 1938, and is a mainstay on most tiki bar menus. Beach was a pioneer when it came to using fresh herbs in his cocktails, something we can be truly thankful for.

Serves 1

60 ml (2 fl oz/¼ cup) white rum
3 teaspoons peach liqueur
¼ cup diced pineapple
45 ml (1½ fl oz) freshly squeezed lime juice

3 teaspoons Sugar syrup (page 250)
1 small handful mint, chopped
mint sprig, for garnish

Place the ingredients (except the garnish) in a high-speed blender with 1 cup ice and blend at high speed until smooth.

Pour into a chilled cocktail glass. Garnish with mint.

SHARK'S TOOTH

THE BOILERMAKER OF COCKTAILS – A DELIGHTFULLY SWEET, SHORT COCKTAIL TO SIP ON WHILE ENJOYING A GOOD-QUALITY AGED RUM.

serves 1

30 ml (1 fl oz) good-quality
   aged rum
30 ml (1 fl oz) gold rum
3 teaspoons freshly squeezed
   lime juice
3 teaspoons freshly squeezed
   pineapple juice

3 teaspoons Sugar syrup
   (page 250)
1 teaspoon maraschino cherry
   liqueur (or juice)
maraschino cherry, for garnish

Pour the aged rum into a shot glass or tumbler.

Place the remaining ingredients (except the garnish) in a high-speed blender with ½ cup crushed ice. Blend at high speed for 5 seconds.

Strain into a cocktail glass filled with crushed ice. Garnish with a maraschino cherry with the aged rum on the side.

MONTEGO BAY

Big and boozy, here is a cocktail that can really show off the different styles of rum. The absinthe, allspice dram and grapefruit balance everything out with wonderfully herbaceous and bitter flavours.

Serves 1

20 ml (¾ fl oz) dark rum
20 ml (¾ fl oz) gold rum
20 ml (¾ fl oz) aged rum
1 teaspoon absinthe
3 teaspoons freshly squeezed lime juice
3 teaspoons freshly squeezed grapefruit juice

20 ml (¾ fl oz) Honey syrup (page 253)
1 teaspoon Allspice dram (page 259)
1 dash Orange bitters (page 258)
grapefruit wheel, for garnish

Combine the ingredients (except the garnish) in a cocktail shaker filled with ice. Shake.

Strain into a chilled cocktail glass filled with crushed ice. Garnish with a grapefruit wheel.

SUMATRA KULA

Another of Beach's earliest creations, dating back to the 1930s, the Sumatra Kula is a bit like the man himself: alcoholic and a little bit fruity.

serves 1

45 ml (1½ fl oz) aged rum

30 ml (1 fl oz) rhum agricole (cane juice rum)

3 teaspoons freshly squeezed grapefruit juice

3 teaspoons freshly squeezed lime juice

3 teaspoons freshly squeezed orange juice

3 teaspoons Honey syrup (page 253)

mint sprig and lime wheel, orange wheel or grapefruit wheel (or a combination), for garnish

Combine the ingredients (except the garnish) in a cocktail shaker filled with crushed ice and shake.

Pour the contents of the shaker into a tall glass and top with crushed ice. Garnish with mint and your choice of citrus wheels.

SHONKY DONKEY

A RUMMY VARIATION OF THE MOSCOW MULE, THIS IS THE PERFECT DRINK FOR A HOT SUMMER AFTERNOON. OR MORNING.

Serves 1

1 lime, cut into 8 pieces
1 small handful mint leaves
2 teaspoons Sugar syrup
  (page 250)
60 ml (2 fl oz/¼ cup) spiced rum

100 ml (3½ fl oz) ginger beer
mint sprig and lime wedge, for
  garnish

Muddle the lime and mint in a cocktail shaker. Add the sugar syrup and rum, and 1 cup ice. Shake vigorously.

Pour the contents of the shaker into a copper mug or tall glass and add more ice if needed. Top up with ginger beer.

Garnish with fresh mint and a lime wedge.

LAST RiTES

Drink too many of these and someone might need to read you yours.
This drink is best made with a really good-quality aged rum.

serves 1

90 ml (3 fl oz) aged rum

20 ml (¾ fl oz) freshly squeezed
lime juice

3 teaspoons Passionfruit syrup
(page 256)

1½ teaspoons Velvet falernum
(page 257)

maraschino cherry, for garnish

Place the ingredients (except the garnish) in a high-speed blender
with 1 cup crushed ice. Blend at high speed for 5 seconds.

Pour into a tall glass and top with crushed ice. Garnish with
a maraschino cherry.

MOONKIST COCONUT

NOTHING SAYS 'HOLIDAY IN PARADISE' LIKE A COCONUT WITH A STRAW STICKING OUT OF IT. THE PROBLEM WITH MOST COCONUTS THOUGH, IS THAT THEY DON'T HAVE ANY RUM IN THEM.

Serves 1

45 ml (1½ fl oz) white rum
20 ml (¾ fl oz) gold rum
1½ teaspoons coconut rum
3 teaspoons freshly squeezed
   lime juice
30 ml (1 fl oz) Rich honey syrup
   (page 253)
2 teaspoons Velvet falernum
   (page 257)

45 ml (1½ fl oz) coconut milk
3 teaspoons coconut cream
2 dashes Orange bitters (page 258)
opened coconut, for serving
   (optional)
pineapple leaves, for garnish

Place the ingredients (except the coconut and garnish) in a high-speed blender with 1 cup crushed ice. Blend at high speed for 5 seconds.

Pour into a coconut (or a large cocktail glass) and garnish with pineapple leaves.

COBRA'S FANG

ONE FROM DON THE BEACHCOMBER'S LIST, THIS SPICY LITTLE SNAKE HAS A REAL BITE. THE PERNOD (OR ABSINTHE), BITTERS AND FALERNUM ADD SOME REALLY NICE HERBACEOUS QUALITIES.

SERVES 1

- 3 teaspoons dark rum
- 30 ml (1 fl oz) 151 proof rum
- 2 teaspoons Pernod or absinthe
- 3 teaspoons freshly squeezed lime juice
- 3 teaspoons freshly squeezed orange juice
- 3 teaspoons Velvet falernum (page 257)
- 3 teaspoons Grenadine (page 251)
- 1 dash Orange bitters (page 258)
- cinnamon stick, for garnish

Place the ingredients (except the garnish) in a high-speed blender with ½ cup crushed ice. Blend at high speed for 5 seconds.

Pour into an old fashioned glass and top with crushed ice. Garnish with a cinnamon stick.

SHRUNKEN SKULL

Just like a regular skull, but smaller! This is a short and sweet way to drink rum.

Serves 1

30 ml (1 fl oz) white rum
30 ml (1 fl oz) demerara rum
30 ml (1 fl oz) Grenadine
 (page 251)

30 ml (1 fl oz) freshly squeezed
 lime juice
pomegranate seeds, for garnish

Combine the ingredients (except the garnish) in a cocktail shaker filled with ice. Shake.

Strain into a skull-shaped tiki mug or old fashioned glass filled with ice. Garnish with pomegranate seeds.

BLUE HAWAIIAN

Didn't we love a blue drink in the old days? You don't see a lot of blue curaçao these days, and that's probably because it adds very little to a drink except the gaudy colour. This recipe is the drink version of that really loud shirt you wore in the 1990s.

Serves 1

30 ml (1 fl oz) white rum
30 ml (1 fl oz) vodka
3 teaspoons blue curaçao
90 ml (3 fl oz) pineapple juice, fresh if possible
30 ml (1 fl oz) freshly squeezed lime juice

3 teaspoons Sugar syrup (page 250)
pineapple wedge, maraschino cherry and cocktail umbrella, for garnish

Combine the ingredients (except the garnish) in a cocktail shaker filled with ice. Shake.

Strain into a tall glass filled with ice and garnish with a pineapple wedge, maraschino cherry and cocktail umbrella.

BEACHCOMBER'S PUNCH

DONN BEACH'S CLASSIC RECIPE FROM THE EARLY DAYS OF TIKI.

serves 1

60 ml (2 fl oz/¼ cup) demerara rum

3 teaspoons apricot brandy

1 teaspoon Pernod

3 teaspoons freshly squeezed lime juice

3 teaspoons freshly squeezed grapefruit juice

3 teaspoons Sugar syrup (page 250)

1 dash Orange bitters (page 258)

mint sprig and cocktail umbrella, for garnish

Place the ingredients (except the garnish) in a high-speed blender with crushed ice. Blend at high speed for 5 seconds.

Pour into a chilled tall glass and top up with more crushed ice if necessary. Garnish with mint and a cocktail umbrella.

MOJITO

ANOTHER FANTASTIC DRINK FROM OUR GOOD FRIENDS IN CUBA.

serves 1

½ lime, cut into 6 pieces
1 small handful mint leaves
3 teaspoons sugar
60 ml (2 fl oz/¼ cup) dark
   Cuban rum

45 ml (1½ fl oz) soda water
   (seltzer).
mint sprig and lime wedge,
   for garnish

Muddle the lime, mint and sugar in a cocktail shaker. Add the rum
and fill the shaker with ice. Shake vigorously.

Pour the contents of the shaker into a tall glass and top with the soda
water. Garnish with mint and a lime wedge.

PINEAPPLE MOJITO

THIS IS A DRINK TO SHARE WITH ANOTHER AS YOU LAZE IN A HAMMOCK
UNDER THE SHADE OF A PALM TREE.

Serves 1

1 lime, cut into 12 pieces
160 g (5½ oz/1 cup) chopped fresh
   pineapple
1 small handful basil leaves
90 ml (3 fl oz) white rum
30 ml (1 fl oz) Sugar syrup
   (page 250)

60 ml (2 fl oz/¼ cup) soda water
   (seltzer)
hollowed-out pineapple, for serving
   (optional)
lemongrass stalk, for garnish

Muddle the lime, pineapple and basil in a cocktail shaker. Add the rum
and sugar syrup, and fill the shaker with crushed ice. Shake vigorously.

Pour the contents of the shaker into a hollowed-out pineapple (or a very
large glass) and top up with crushed ice and the soda water. Garnish
with lemongrass and two straws.

BLUEBERRY MOJITO

OTHERWISE KNOWN AS THE 'HOMEOWNER'S MOJITO' DUE TO THE EXORBITANT PRICE OF BLUEBERRIES.

SERVES 1

1 lime, cut into 12 pieces
155 g (5½ oz/1 cup) fresh
  blueberries, plus extra for garnish
1 small handful mint leaves
45 ml (1½ fl oz) white rum
30 ml (1 fl oz) umeshu (Japanese
  plum wine)

30 ml (1 fl oz) Sugar Syrup
  (page 250)
60 ml (2 fl oz/¼ cup) soda water
  (seltzer)
lime wedge, for garnish

Muddle the lime, blueberries and mint in a cocktail shaker. Add the rum, umeshu and sugar syrup. Fill the shaker with ice and shake vigorously.

Pour the contents of the shaker into a tall glass and top up with ice. Add the soda water. Garnish with blueberries and a lime wedge.

FREMANTLE DOCTOR

COOL AND REFRESHING IN THE AFTERNOON. THIS IS ONE DOCTOR I'M HAPPY
TO KEEP REVISITING.

Serves 1

30 ml (1 fl oz) white rum

3 teaspoons apricot brandy

30 ml (1 fl oz) freshly squeezed
lemon juice

90 ml (3 fl oz) pineapple juice,
fresh if possible

3 teaspoons Galliano

blood orange wheel and
maraschino cherry, for garnish

Combine the rum, brandy and fruit juices in a cocktail shaker filled with
ice. Shake.

Strain into a tall glass filled with ice. Float the Galliano on top by pouring
it over the back of a spoon.

Garnish with a blood orange wheel and a maraschino cherry.

BEHIND THE BIKE SHED

THIS DRINK IS FULL OF PASSION. SHARE WITH A CLOSE FRIEND.

serves 2

60 ml (2 fl oz/¼ cup) white rum
60 ml (2 fl oz/¼ cup) gold rum
60 ml (2 fl oz/¼ cup) freshly
squeezed pink grapefruit juice
90 ml (3 fl oz) pineapple juice,
fresh if possible
3 teaspoons Passionfruit syrup
(page 256)

60 ml (2 fl oz/¼ cup) lemonade
1 teaspoon maraschino cherry
liqueur (or juice)
maraschino cherries and finger
lime, for garnish

Combine the rums, fruit juices and passionfruit syrup in a cocktail shaker
filled with ice. Shake.

Strain into two tall glasses filled with ice. Top with the lemonade and
maraschino liqueur.

Garnish with maraschino cherries and finger lime.

RUM 'N' RASPBERRIES

I LOVE A GOOD RASPBERRY. I'M ALSO A HUGE FAN OF RUM. IMAGINE MY
DELIGHT WHEN I WRAP MY LIPS AROUND THIS LITTLE BEAUTY.

serves 1

60 g (2 oz/½ cup) fresh raspberries,
  plus extra for garnish
45 ml (1½ fl oz) spiced rum
3 teaspoons raspberry liqueur

3 teaspoons lime juice
1 dash Orange bitters (page 258)
2 teaspoons agave syrup

Muddle the raspberries in a cocktail shaker. Add the remaining
ingredients (except the garnish) along with ½ cup ice. Shake vigorously.

Pour the contents of the shaker into an old fashioned glass and top
with ice if necessary. Garnish with fresh raspberries.

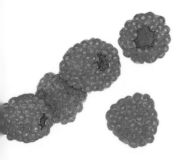

BiG BAMBOO LOVE SONG

LEMONGRASS SHOULD BE USED IN MORE COCKTAILS. NOT ONLY DOES IT ADD A GREAT ZESTY FLAVOUR, BUT IT ALSO MAKES A GREAT SWIZZLE STICK FOR STIRRING YOUR DRINK.

serves 1

60 ml (2 fl oz/¼ cup) dark rum
30 ml (1 fl oz) white rum
3 teaspoons orange curaçao
30 ml (1 fl oz) freshly squeezed
   orange juice
60 ml (2 fl oz/¼ cup) pineapple
   juice, fresh if possible

30 ml (1 fl oz) freshly squeezed
   lime juice
bruised lemongrass stalk,
   for garnish

Combine the ingredients (except the garnish) in a cocktail shaker filled with ice. Shake.

Strain into a tall glass filled with crushed ice. Garnish with a bruised lemongrass stalk.

JAMAICAN ME CRAZY

Drink enough of these and you probably will go a little troppo.

serves 1

30 ml (1 fl oz) Jamaican rum
30 ml (1 fl oz) coconut rum
3 teaspoons banana liqueur
2 teaspoons Grenadine
   (page 251)

30 ml (1 fl oz) pineapple juice, fresh
   if possible
30 ml (1 fl oz) cranberry juice
lime wheel, for garnish

Place the ingredients (except the garnish) in a high-speed blender with 1 cup ice and blend at high speed until smooth.

Pour into a hurricane glass and garnish with a lime wheel.

BLUE MULLET

I'M UNSURE AS TO WHETHER THIS DRINK WAS NAMED AFTER A FISH OR BILLY RAY CYRUS' HAIR AFTER A BAD DYE JOB.

serves 1

45 ml (1½ fl oz) white rum
3 teaspoons coconut rum
2 teaspoons blue curaçao
2 teaspoons freshly squeezed lime juice
2 teaspoons freshly squeezed lemon juice

2 teaspoons Sugar syrup (page 250)
30 ml (1 fl oz) freshly squeezed orange juice
maraschino cherry, for garnish

Combine the ingredients (except the garnish) in a cocktail shaker filled with ice. Shake.

Strain into an old fashioned glass filled with ice. Garnish with a maraschino cherry.

CARIBBEAN SUNSET

WHEN THE SUN GOES DOWN IN THE CARIBBEAN, YOU KNOW IT'S TIME TO ORDER ANOTHER COCKTAIL.

serves 1

45 ml (1½ fl oz) white rum

3 teaspoons coconut rum

60 ml (2 fl oz/¼ cup) pineapple juice, fresh if possible

60 ml (2 fl oz/¼ cup) freshly squeezed orange juice

3 teaspoons Grenadine (page 251)

pineapple wedge, for garnish

Combine the rums and fruit juices in a cocktail shaker filled with ice. Shake.

Strain into a tall glass filled with ice. Add the grenadine and garnish with a pineapple wedge.

CARIBBEAN ISLAND
ICED COFFEE

The caffeinated cousin of the Long Island Iced Tea. Put this in
a takeaway coffee cup and you can get drunk at work without
anyone knowing!

Serves 1

30 ml (1 fl oz) Jamaican rum
30 ml (1 fl oz) white rum
3 teaspoons coffee liqueur

20 ml (¾ fl oz) sweetened
  condensed milk
90 ml (3 fl oz) espresso, chilled
coffee beans, for garnish

Combine the ingredients (except the garnish) in a cocktail shaker filled
with ice. Shake.

Strain into a tall glass filled with ice. Garnish with coffee beans.

RUM DADDY

When I was a child, the first words to come out of my mouth were, 'Rum, daddy!'

Serves 1

60 ml (2 fl oz/¼ cup) aged rum
3 teaspoons Pernod
3 teaspoons Velvet Falernum (page 257)
30 ml (1 fl oz) Sugar syrup (page 250)

30 ml (1 fl oz) freshly squeezed lime juice
2 dashes Orange bitters (page 258)
orange wheel, for garnish

Combine the ingredients (except the garnish) in a cocktail shaker filled with ice. Shake.

Strain into a highball glass filled with crushed ice. Garnish with an orange wheel.

MENEHUNE JUICE

'You can't see or talk to a Menehune until you drink some Menehune Juice. So drink some.' – Trader Vic

Serves 1

60 ml (2 fl oz/¼ cup) white rum

3 teaspoons orange curaçao

2 teaspoons Orgeat syrup (page 252)

2 teaspoons Sugar syrup (page 250)

30 ml (1 fl oz) freshly squeezed lime juice

mint sprig and lime wheel, for garnish

Combine the ingredients (except the garnish) in a cocktail shaker filled with crushed ice. Shake.

Strain into a tall glass and top with crushed ice. Garnish with mint and a lime wheel.

KONA GOLD

A FEW THINGS HAVE BEEN NAMED KONA GOLD: A RACEHORSE; A BRAND OF COFFEE; A CERTAIN HAWAIIAN STRAIN OF SATIVA THAT CAN, ALLEGEDLY, GIVE YOU SOARING CEREBRAL EUPHORIA … AND THIS DRINK.

Serves 1

60 ml (2 fl oz/¼ cup) gold rum
1 teaspoon maraschino cherry
   liqueur (or juice)

30 ml (1 fl oz) Don's mix (page 261)
3 teaspoons Pernod
maraschino cherry, for garnish

Combine the rum, cherry liqueur and Don's mix in a cocktail shaker filled with ice. Shake.

Strain into an old fashioned glass filled with crushed ice. Float the Pernod on top by pouring it over the back of a spoon.

Garnish with a maraschino cherry.

LAPU LAPU

THIS DRINK IS SO GOOD THEY NAMED IT TWICE.

serves 1

60 ml (2 fl oz/¼ cup) dark rum

30 ml (1 fl oz) pineapple juice, fresh if possible

60 ml (2 fl oz/¼ cup) freshly squeezed orange juice

3 teaspoons freshly squeezed lime juice

3 teaspoons freshly squeezed lemon juice

3 teaspoons Sugar syrup (page 250)

3 teaspoons 151 proof rum

pineapple wedge, lemon wheel and lime twist, for garnish

Combine the dark rum, fruit juices and sugar syrup in a cocktail shaker filled with ice. Shake.

Strain into a highball glass filled with ice. Float the 151 proof rum on top by pouring it over the back of a spoon.

Garnish with a pineapple wedge, lemon wheel and lime twist and drink through a straw.

POMME AND CINNAMONY

APPLE AND CINNAMON MAKE FOR GREAT BEDFELLOWS UNDER A SHEET OF
PASTRY, WHY NOT TRY THEM IN A DELICIOUS COCKTAIL?

serves 1–2

30 ml (1 fl oz) white rum
30 ml (1 fl oz) gold rum
3 teaspoons freshly squeezed
lime juice
3 teaspoons Cinnamon syrup

60 ml (2 fl oz/¼ cup) cloudy
apple juice
apple slices and ground cinnamon,
for garnish

Combine the ingredients (except the garnish) in a cocktail shaker filled
with ice. Shake.

Strain into a highball glass filled with ice. Garnish with apple slices and
a dusting of cinnamon.

VIRGIN SACRIFICE

POOR VIRGINS. IN THE OLD DAYS THEY WERE ALWAYS GETTING SACRIFICED.
I CAN'T EVEN REMEMBER A TIME WHEN THAT WOULD HAVE BEEN AN ISSUE
FOR ME ...

Serves 1

60 ml (2 fl oz/¼ cup) gold rum
3 teaspoons coconut rum
90 ml (3 fl oz) guava juice
30 ml (1 fl oz) pineapple juice,
   fresh if possible

3 teaspoons freshly squeezed
   lime juice
2 teaspoons Sugar syrup
   (page 250)
maraschino cherry, for garnish

Combine the ingredients (except the garnish) in a cocktail shaker filled
with ice. Shake.

Strain into a highball glass filled with crushed ice. Garnish with a
maraschino cherry.

GLASS SLiPPER

Sip this liquor, this glass slipper, by midnight you'll be drunken, and be turned into a pumpkin.

serves 1

60 ml (2 fl oz/¼ cup) rhum agricole (sugar cane rum)

20 ml (¾ fl oz) elderflower liqueur

20 ml (¾ fl oz) lemon juice

3 teaspoons Vanilla syrup (page 254)

2 teaspoons 151 proof rum

edible flowers, for garnish

Combine the rhum agricole, elderflower liqueur, lemon juice and vanilla syrup in a cocktail shaker filled with ice. Shake.

Strain into an old fashioned glass filled with crushed ice. Float the 151 proof rum on top by pouring it over the back of a spoon. Garnish with edible flowers.

PUNKY MONKEY

Spices are awesome. They do nice things in your mouth.

serves 1

3 cardamom pods
30 ml (1 fl oz) aged rum
30 ml (1 fl oz) bourbon
3 teaspoons agave nectar
3 teaspoons pineapple juice, fresh
if possible

3 teaspoons freshly squeezed
lemon juice
1 dash Orange bitters (page 258)
star anise, for garnish

Muddle the cardamom pods in a cocktail shaker. Add the remaining ingredients (except the garnish) and fill the shaker with ice. Shake vigorously.

Strain into a chilled cocktail glass and garnish with star anise.

POTTED PARROT

A NUTTY LITTLE NUMBER THAT WILL HAVE YOU CHIRPING ALL NIGHT UNTIL YOU DROP OFF YOUR PERCH.

Serves 1

60 ml (2 fl oz/¼ cup) white rum
3 teaspoons orange curaçao
60 ml (2 fl oz/¼ cup) freshly squeezed orange juice
30 ml (1 fl oz) freshly squeezed lemon juice

2 teaspoons Orgeat syrup (page 252)
2 teaspoons Sugar syrup (page 250)
mint sprig, for garnish

Combine the ingredients (except the garnish) in a cocktail shaker filled with ice. Shake.

Strain into an old fashioned glass filled with ice. Garnish with mint.

QUEEN'S PARK SWIZZLE

This little swizzle is named after the Queen's Park Hotel in Trinidad where it was created in the 1920s. Simple and delicious.

Serves 1

3 teaspoons freshly squeezed lime juice

2 sprigs mint, plus extra to garnish

60 ml (2 fl oz/¼ cup) dark rum

2 dashes Orange bitters (page 258)

3 teaspoons Sugar syrup (page 250)

60 ml (2 fl oz/¼ cup) soda water (seltzer)

Place the lime juice and mint in a metal cup. Fill with crushed ice.

Add the rum, bitters and sugar syrup. Stir to combine and top with soda. Garnish with mint.

MARTINIQUE SWIZZLE

This drink is to be stirred, not shaken. That's what makes it a swizzle.

serves 1

60 ml (2 fl oz/¼ cup) Martinique gold rum

2 teaspoons Pernod

3 teaspoons freshly squeezed lime juice

2 teaspoons Sugar syrup (page 250)

2 dashes Orange bitters (page 258)

mint sprig and lime wheel, for garnish

Combine the ingredients (except the garnish) in a highball glass filled with crushed ice and stir to combine.

Garnish with mint and a lime wheel.

MOLOKAI MIKE

One of Trader Vic's concoctions. This drink should be in a fancy-looking glass to show off the layered colours.

serves 1

30 ml (1 fl oz) white rum
3 teaspoons brandy
30 ml (1 fl oz) freshly squeezed orange juice
30 ml (1 fl oz) freshly squeezed lemon juice

3 teaspoons Orgeat syrup (page 252)
3 teaspoons dark rum
2 teaspoons Grenadine (page 251)
orange wheel and lemon wheel, for garnish

Combine the white rum, brandy, fruit juices and orgeat syrup in a cocktail shaker filled with ice. Shake.

Strain into a fancy-looking glass half-filled with crushed ice.

Combine the dark rum and grenadine in a cocktail shaker with ½ cup crushed ice and shake.

Gently pour into the glass to layer. Garnish with an orange wheel and a lemon wheel.

RUMBLE iN THE JUNGLE

WITH FOUR DIFFERENT RUMS, THIS HEAVYWEIGHT PACKS A PUNCH. ARE YOU READY TO RUMBLE?

serves 1

30 ml (1 fl oz) spiced rum
3 teaspoons coconut rum
3 teaspoons dark rum
3 teaspoons white rum
60 ml (2 fl oz/¼ cup) freshly squeezed orange juice

60 ml (2 fl oz/¼ cup) pineapple juice, fresh if possible
3 teaspoons Grenadine (page 251)
pineapple wedge and orange wheel, for garnish

Place the ingredients (except the garnish) in a high-speed blender with 1 cup crushed ice. Blend at high speed for 5 seconds.

Pour into a tall glass and garnish with a pineapple wedge and orange wheel.

FLYING DUTCHMAN

THE FLYING DUTCHMAN WAS A LEGENDARY GHOST SHIP, DOOMED TO SAIL THE SEVEN SEAS FOR ALL ETERNITY, COMMUNICATING ONLY WITH THE DEAD. THIS DRINK, HOWEVER, IS A DELIGHTFUL MIX OF RUM AND CRANBERRY JUICE, AND WILL ONLY HAVE YOU COMMUNING WITH THE DEAD IF YOU SERIOUSLY OVERDO IT.

Serves 1

30 ml (1 fl oz) dark rum
30 ml (1 fl oz) rhum agricole
  (cane juice rum)
45 ml (1½ fl oz) cranberry juice
3 teaspoons pineapple juice, fresh
  if possible

2 teaspoons Grenadine
  (page 251)
2 dashes Orange bitters (page 258)
mint sprig, for garnish

Combine the ingredients (except the garnish) in a cocktail shaker filled with ice. Shake.

Strain into a tall glass filled with ice. Garnish with mint.

LUCY LOU

THIS GROWN-UP SMOOTHIE IS GREAT AFTER A WORKOUT OR IF YOU MISS BREAKFAST. WHAT? DON'T YOU NEED A STIFF DRINK AFTER THE HORRORS OF EXERCISE?

Serves 1

30 ml (1 fl oz) aged rum
45 ml (1½ fl oz) cream liqueur
3 teaspoons oloroso sherry
¼ banana

3 teaspoons Sugar syrup
(page 250)
pinch of salt
tropical flower and vanilla beans,
for garnish

Place the ingredients (except the garnish) in a high-speed blender with 1 cup crushed ice. Blend at high speed for 5 seconds.

Pour into a poco grande glass. Garnish with a tropical flower and vanilla beans.

HUKILAU

Spices from the rum, heat from the ginger and a nuttiness from the amaretto make for a very unique drink.

serves 1

30 ml (1 fl oz) spiced rum
3 teaspoons ginger liqueur
2 teaspoons amaretto
60 ml (2 fl oz/¼ cup) pineapple
    juice, fresh if possible

30 ml (1 fl oz) freshly squeezed
    orange juice
3 teaspoons freshly squeezed lime
    juice
orange wheel and lime wedge,
    for garnish

Combine the ingredients (except the garnish) in a cocktail shaker filled with ice. Shake.

Strain into an old fashioned glass filled with ice. Garnish with an orange wheel and a lime wedge.

SiBONEY

MUCH LIKE THE CLASSIC CUBAN SONG IT IS NAMED AFTER, THIS DRINK IS
FULL OF PASSION ... FRUIT SYRUP. OH, AND RUM.

serves 1

30 ml (1 fl oz) dark rum
30 ml (1 fl oz) white rum
3 teaspoons lemon juice
3 teaspoons Passionfruit syrup
(page 256)

3 teaspoons pineapple juice, fresh
if possible
pineapple wedge and maraschino
cherry, for garnish

Combine the ingredients (except the garnish) in a cocktail shaker filled
with ice. Shake.

Strain into a chilled cocktail glass. Garnish with a pineapple wedge and
maraschino cherry.

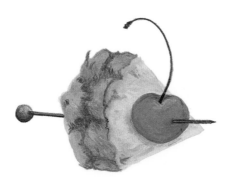

TABU

A FRESH-FLAVOURED SLUSHY THAT WILL DO YOU VERY NICELY ON A HOT SUMMER'S DAY.

serves 1

60 ml (2 fl oz/¼ cup) rhum agricole (cane juice rum)

90 ml (3 fl oz) pineapple juice, fresh if possible

30 ml (1 fl oz) cranberry juice

3 teaspoons Sugar syrup (page 250)

3 teaspoons freshly squeezed lemon juice

6 mint leaves

mint sprig, for garnish

Place the ingredients (except the garnish) in a high-speed blender with 1 cup ice. Blend at high speed until smooth.

Pour into a hurricane glass and garnish with mint.

TAHITIAN GOLD

Tahitian limes and gold rum... gee, they really put a lot of thought into naming this drink.

serves 1

60 ml (2 fl oz/¼ cup) gold rum
1 teaspoon maraschino cherry
   liqueur (or juice)
30 ml (1 fl oz) freshly squeezed
   lime juice

3 teaspoons Sugar syrup
   (page 250)
1 teaspoon Pernod

Combine the ingredients (except the Pernod) in a cocktail shaker filled with ice. Shake.

Strain into a chilled cocktail glass and float the Pernod on top by pouring it over the back of a spoon.

BARREL O' RUM

WHAT'S MORE FUN THAN A BARREL O' MONKEYS? THE ANSWER IS A BARREL O' RUM.

serves 1

60 ml (2 fl oz/¼ cup) white rum

60 ml (2 fl oz/¼ cup) dark rum

60 ml (2 fl oz/¼ cup) freshly squeezed lime juice

60 ml (2 fl oz/¼ cup) freshly squeezed orange juice

60 ml (2 fl oz/¼ cup) freshly squeezed grapefruit juice

60 ml (2 fl oz/¼ cup) Passionfruit syrup (page 256)

1 teaspoon Rich honey syrup (page 253)

3 teaspoons soda water (seltzer)

1 teaspoon Orange bitters (page 258)

½ passionfruit

2 teaspoons 151 proof rum

Place the white and dark rum, fruit juices, syrups, soda water and bitters in a high-speed blender with 1 cup crushed ice. Blend at high speed for 5 seconds.

Pour into a ceramic rum barrel mug or large brandy balloon. Top with the half passionfruit. Pour in the 151 proof rum and carefully ignite.

FOG CUTTER

The origin of this classic tiki cocktail is disputed as to whether Donn Beach or Trader Vic invented it. Either way, it's a great cocktail that changes subtly as you get towards the end and the amontillado sherry comes into play – definitely a drink to be drunk through a big curly straw.

Serves 1

60 ml (2 fl oz/¼ cup) white rum
30 ml (1 fl oz) brandy or cognac
3 teaspoons dry gin
60 ml (2 fl oz/¼ cup) freshly squeezed lemon juice
30 ml (1 fl oz) freshly squeezed orange juice

3 teaspoons Orgeat syrup (page 252)
3 teaspoons amontillado sherry
orange wheel and maraschino cherry, for garnish

Combine the rum, brandy or cognac, gin, fruit juices and orgeat syrup in a cocktail shaker filled with ice. Shake.

Strain into a tall glass filled with ice. Float the sherry on top by pouring it over the back of a spoon. Garnish with an orange wheel and a maraschino cherry.

FULL MOON PARTY

Turn the music up, close your eyes and drink deeply. You can almost feel the sand between your toes and smell the backpackers.

serves 1

60 ml (2 fl oz/¼ cup) dark rum
3 teaspoons absinthe
60 ml (2 fl oz/¼ cup) freshly
   squeezed lime juice
3 teaspoons freshly squeezed
   lemon juice

3 teaspoons Grenadine
   (page 251)
90 ml (3 fl oz) soda water (seltzer)
lime wheel, for garnish

Combine the ingredients (except the soda water and garnish) in a cocktail shaker filled with ice. Shake.

Strain into a tall glass filled with crushed ice. Top with the soda water and garnish with a lime wheel.

THE CASTAWAY

For when you want to get wrecked. Best enjoyed in the company of a volleyball.

Serves 1

30 ml (1 fl oz) gold rum

30 ml (1 fl oz) amaretto

60 ml (2 fl oz/¼ cup) pineapple juice, fresh if possible

3 teaspoons freshly squeezed lime juice

2 teaspoons coconut cream

2 teaspoons Sugar syrup (page 250)

2 dashes Orange bitters (page 258)

maraschino cherries, for garnish

Combine the ingredients (except the garnish) in a cocktail shaker filled with ice. Shake.

Strain into a tall glass filled with ice. Garnish with maraschino cherries.

BEACHCOMBER'S GOLD

ALMOST A RUM-BASED MANHATTAN, THIS IS ONE FROM DON THE
BEACHCOMBER'S. THIS DRINK WAS ORIGINALLY SERVED IN A MOULDED
ICE BLOCK. TRY IT AT HOME!

Serves 1

30 ml (1 fl oz) aged rum
30 ml (1 fl oz) white rum
3 teaspoons sweet vermouth

3 teaspoons dry vermouth
1 dash Orange bitters (page 258)
orange slice and maraschino
cherry, for garnish

Combine the ingredients (except the garnish) in a cocktail shaker filled
with ice and stir vigorously.

Strain into a chilled cocktail glass. Garnish with an orange slice and
a maraschino cherry.

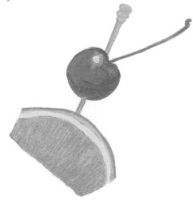

MARA AMU

A MODERN TIKI COCKTAIL INVENTED BY MAI KAI RESTAURANT IN FORT LAUDERDALE IN FLORIDA. THIS DRINK IS SO POPULAR IT HAS IT'S OWN TIKI MUG.

Serves 1

3 teaspoons white rum
3 teaspoons gold rum
3 teaspoons dark rum
20 ml (¾ fl oz) freshly squeezed lime juice
20 ml (¾ fl oz) freshly squeezed orange juice
20 ml (¾ fl oz) freshly squeezed grapefruit juice
20 ml (¾ fl oz) Passionfruit syrup (page 256)
pink grapefruit wedge, for garnish

Place the ingredients (except the garnish) in a high-speed blender with 1 cup crushed ice. Blend at high speed for 5 seconds.

Pour into a Mara Amu mug or tall glass. Garnish with a pink grapefruit wedge.

SNAKE TEMPLE

Sloe gin is made by infusing regular gin with sloe berries, much like gold rum is infused with actual gold... Sure, okay that's not true but I had you there for a second, right?

serves 1

30 ml (1 fl oz) gold rum
30 ml (1 fl oz) rhum agricole
 (cane juice rum)
3 teaspoons sloe gin

20 ml (¾ fl oz) freshly squeezed
 lime juice
3 teaspoons Velvet falernum
 (page 257)
lime wheel, for garnish

Combine the ingredients (except the garnish) in a cocktail shaker filled with ice. Shake.

Strain into a tall glass filled with crushed ice. Garnish with a lime wheel.

Tiki Boom Boom

More coloured layers! Red, yellow and blue like the colours of Venezuela, only in a different order, most likely because this drink is not from there. Looks pretty though!

serves 1

30 ml (1 fl oz) white rum
3 teaspoons coconut rum
3 teaspoons pineapple rum
80 ml (2½ fl oz/⅓ cup) coconut water
3 teaspoons freshly squeezed
  lemon juice

3 teaspoons Sugar syrup
  (page 250)
2 teaspoons Grenadine
  (page 251)
2 teaspoons blue curaçao
maraschino cherry, for garnish

Combine the rums, coconut water, lemon juice and sugar syrup in a cocktail shaker filled with ice, and shake vigorously.

Pour the grenadine into a poco grande glass and fill with crushed ice. Strain the rum mixture slowly into the glass and float the blue curaçao on top by pouring it over the back of a spoon.

Garnish with a maraschino cherry.

EL PRESIDENTE

Vote for Pedro.

serves 1

45 ml (1½ fl oz) white rum
45 ml (1½ fl oz) dry vermouth
1 teaspoon orange curaçao

½ teaspoon Grenadine (page 251)
orange twist and maraschino
cherry, for garnish

Pour the ingredients (except the garnish) into a cocktail shaker filled with ice and stir vigorously.

Strain into a chilled cocktail glass.

Squeeze the orange twist over the drink to release the oils from the skin. Rub the rind along the rim of the glass. Drop the twist into the glass along with a maraschino cherry.

TORTUGA

This has a lot of over-proofed rum. Don't lose your head.

Serves 1

45 ml (1½ fl oz) 151 proof rum
30 ml (1 fl oz) sweet vermouth
2 teaspoons orange curaçao
45 ml (1½ fl oz) freshly squeezed
    orange juice
3 teaspoons freshly squeezed
    lime juice

30 ml (1 fl oz) freshly squeezed
    lemon juice
2 teaspoons Grenadine
    (page 251)
mint sprig and orange wheel,
    for garnish

Place the ingredients (except the garnish) in a high-speed blender filled
with ice. Blend at high speed until smooth.

Pour into a double old fashioned glass and garnish with mint and an
orange wheel.

RUM RUNNER

You won't be doing any running after you've smuggled a couple of these bad boys.

serves 1

30 ml (1 fl oz) dark rum
30 ml (1 fl oz) white rum
30 ml (1 fl oz) blackberry liqueur
30 ml (1 fl oz) banana liqueur
30 ml (1 fl oz) freshly squeezed orange juice
30 ml (1 fl oz) pineapple juice, fresh if possible

2 teaspoons Grenadine (page 251)
3 teaspoons 151 proof white rum (optional)
orange slice and cocktail umbrella, for garnish

Place the dark and white rums, the liqueurs and the fruit juices in a high-speed blender with 1 cup ice. Blend until smooth.

Pour into a hurricane glass and add the grenadine. If using, float the 151 proof rum on top by pouring it over the back of a spoon.

Garnish with an orange slice and cocktail umbrella.

JUNGLE BiRD

Sophisticated and colourful – like a toucan in a waistcoat.

serves 1

45 ml (1½ fl oz) gold rum
3 teaspoons dark rum
20 ml (¾ fl oz) Campari
45 ml (1½ fl oz) pineapple juice, fresh if possible

3 teaspoons freshly squeezed lime juice
3 teaspoons Sugar syrup (page 250)
orange wheel, for garnish

Combine the ingredients (except the garnish) in a cocktail shaker filled with ice. Shake.

Strain into an old fashioned glass filled with ice. Garnish with an orange wheel.

ALOHA

Is it me you're looking for?

Serves 1

3 teaspoons dark rum
2 teaspoons dry vermouth
2 teaspoons brandy or cognac
2 teaspoons gin

3 teaspoons freshly squeezed
 lime juice
30 ml (1 fl oz) soda water (seltzer)
lime wheel, for garnish

Combine the ingredients (except the garnish) in a cocktail shaker filled
with ice. Shake.

Strain into a chilled cocktail glass and garnish with a lime wheel.

AKU AKU

THE NAME OF THIS DRINK REFERS TO THE CARVED STONE HEADS FOUND SCATTERED AROUND EASTER ISLAND. LEGEND SAYS THAT HE WHO DRINKS THIS DRINK BECOMES STONY-FACED AND MYSTERIOUS.

SERVES 1

30 ml (1 fl oz) white rum

3 teaspoons peach liqueur

3 teaspoons freshly squeezed lime juice

60 g (2 oz/⅓ cup) chopped pineapple

1 small handful mint leaves

3 teaspoons Sugar syrup (page 250)

mint sprig and pineapple wedge, for garnish

Place the ingredients (except the garnish) in a high-speed blender with 1½ cups crushed ice. Blend until smooth.

Pour into an old fashioned glass and garnish with mint and a pineapple wedge.

SNEAKY TiKi

BEST DRUNK THROUGH A STRAW WITH MINIMAL STIRRING, THIS ONE CREEPS UP ON YOU AS YOU GET CLOSER TO THE BOTTOM.

serves 1

60 ml (2 fl oz/¼ cup) white rum
3 teaspoons blue curaçao
30 ml (1 fl oz) mango juice
30 ml (1 fl oz) guava juice
3 teaspoons pineapple juice

3 teaspoons freshly squeezed lime juice
3 teaspoons aged rum
lime wheel, for garnish

Combine the white rum, blue curaçao and fruit juices in a cocktail shaker filled with ice. Shake.

Strain into a hurricane glass filled with ice. Float the aged rum on top by pouring it over the back of a spoon. Garnish with a lime wheel.

iSLAND HOLiDAY

For when you're not sure exactly where you want to go, but you know you want something tropical.

serves 1

30 ml (1 fl oz) white rum
3 teaspoons mango liqueur
3 teaspoons melon liqueur
3 teaspoons banana liqueur
60 ml (2 fl oz/¼ cup) freshly
   squeezed pink grapefruit juice

60 ml (2 fl oz/¼ cup) soda water
   (seltzer)
3 teaspoons cranberry juice
pineapple leaves, for garnish

Pour the rum, liqueurs and grapefruit juice into a tall glass. Stir to combine.

Fill the glass with ice and top with soda and cranberry juice.

Garnish with pineapple leaves.

iSLAND BREEZE

As refreshing as it sounds.

serves 1

60 ml (2 fl oz/¼ cup) white rum
30 ml (1 fl oz) cranberry juice
100 ml (3½ fl oz) pineapple juice,
  fresh if possible

2 dashes Orange bitters (page 258)
maraschino cherry and lemon
  wheel, for garnish

Combine the rum and cranberry juice in a highball glass filled with ice.

Slowly add the pineapple juice, trying to leave a blush of cranberry at the bottom. Add the bitters.

Garnish with a maraschino cherry and lemon wheel.

COCONUT KiSS

IT'S LIKE BEING A TEENAGER AGAIN, SMEARING ON THAT SWEET, COCONUTTY, CHERRY LIP BALM READY TO BE KISSED. EXCEPT YOU'RE 45 AND COMPLETELY, UTTERLY ALONE.

Serves 1

30 ml (1 fl oz) coconut rum
30 ml (1 fl oz) white rum
20 ml (¾ fl oz) cherry brandy
30 ml (1 fl oz) cream

2 teaspoons Grenadine
(page 251)
maraschino cherry and grated
coconut, for garnish

Combine the ingredients (except the garnish) in a cocktail shaker filled with ice. Shake.

Strain into a chilled cocktail glass and garnish with a maraschino cherry and grated coconut.

OUTRIGGER

AN OUTRIGGER IS A PROJECTING STRUCTURE ON A BOAT, MEANT TO
PROVIDE STABILIZATION. AFTER FOUR OF THESE DRINKS, YOU MIGHT
NEED A PROJECTING STRUCTURE OF YOUR OWN.

serves 1

30 ml (1 fl oz) white rum
30 ml (1 fl oz) gold rum
1½ teaspoons orange curaçao
1½ teaspoons Grenadine
  (page 251)

30 ml (1 fl oz) freshly squeezed
  orange juice
30 ml (1 fl oz) freshly squeezed
  lemon juice
pineapple wedge, to garnish

Combine the ingredients (except the garnish) in a cocktail shaker filled
with ice. Shake.

Strain into a chilled cocktail glass. Garnish with a pineapple wedge.

FIRECRACKER

Set your tiki party off with a bang! Watermelon and chilli make a great combination; add a little rum and you'll really spice up your life.

serves 1

1 lime, cut into 8 pieces
90 g (3 oz/½ cup) chopped fresh watermelon
60 ml (2 fl oz/¼ cup) aged rum
30 ml (1 fl oz) orange curaçao

30 ml (1 fl oz) Sugar syrup (page 250)
1 pinch chilli powder
watermelon wedge and sliced chilli, for garnish

Muddle the lime and watermelon in a cocktail shaker. Add the rum, curaçao, sugar syrup and chilli powder. Fill the shaker with ice and shake vigorously.

Strain into an old fashioned glass filled with ice.

Garnish with a watermelon wedge and sliced chilli.

151 SWiZZLE

THIS SWIZZLE WILL PUT SOME SIZZLE IN YOUR NIZZLE.

Serves 1

45 ml (1½ fl oz) 151 proof
   demerara rum

3 teaspoons freshly squeezed
   lime juice

3 teaspoons Don's mix
   (page 261)

1 dash Orange bitters (page 258)

1 teaspoon Pernod

cinnamon stick, lime wheel and
   freshly grated nutmeg, for garnish

Place the ingredients (except the garnish) in a high-speed blender with
1 cup crushed ice. Blend at high speed for 5 seconds.

Pour into a chilled swizzle or other stainless steel cup and top up with
ice. Garnish with a cinnamon stick, lime wheel and grated nutmeg.

BLACK MAGIC

Now here is a drink to rival the Espresso Martini. It's long, stiff and will keep you up all night. Once you've had Black Magic, there's no going back... Magic...

Serves 1

45 ml (1½ fl oz) dark rum

45 ml (1½ fl oz) aged rum

45 ml (1½ fl oz) freshly brewed espresso

20 ml (¾ fl oz) freshly squeezed lime juice

20 ml (¾ fl oz) freshly squeezed orange juice

20 ml (¾ fl oz) freshly squeezed grapefruit juice

20 ml (¾ fl oz) Rich honey syrup (page 253)

3 teaspoons Don's mix (page 261)

1 dash Vanilla syrup (page 254)

1 dash Allspice dram (page 259)

2 dashes Orange bitters (page 258)

lemon twist, for garnish

Place the ingredients (except the garnish) in a high-speed blender with 1 cup crushed ice. Blend at high speed until frothy.

Pour into a large brandy balloon and garnish with a lemon twist.

MUTINY

IF THE ROYAL NAVY'S WILLIAM BLIGH HAD GIVEN HIS MEN THIS DRINK IN 1789, HE WOULDN'T HAVE HAD HIS FAMOUS MUTINY AND THERE DEFINITELY WOULDN'T HAVE BEEN A RUM REBELLION.

Serves 1

45 ml (1½ fl oz) white rum

45 ml (1½ fl oz) dark rum

20 ml (¾ fl oz) freshly squeezed orange juice

20 ml (¾ fl oz) freshly squeezed lime juice

20 ml (¾ fl oz) freshly squeezed grapefruit juice

3 teaspoons Rich honey syrup (page 253)

3 teaspoons Passionfruit syrup (page 256)

45 ml (1½ fl oz) freshly brewed espresso

2 teaspoons Don's mix (page 261)

2 dashes Orange bitters (page 258)

1 teaspoon Pernod

coffee beans or ground coffee, for garnish

Place the ingredients (except the garnish) in a high-speed blender with 1 cup crushed ice and blend at high speed until frothy.

Pour into a large brandy balloon. Garnish with coffee beans or ground coffee.

VANILLA GORILLA

If you wanna thrill 'er, then fill 'er with a vanilla gorilla! Just don't spill 'er.

Serves 1

30 ml (1 fl oz) white rum
30 ml (1 fl oz) aged rum
3 teaspoons Licor 43
2 teaspoons banana liqueur

20 ml (¾ fl oz) freshly squeezed lime juice
¼ teaspoon vanilla extract
vanilla bean, for garnish

Combine the ingredients (except the garnish) in a cocktail shaker filled with ice. Shake.

Strain into an old fashioned glass filled with crushed ice. Garnish with a vanilla bean.

GOLDEN COLADA

A VARIATION ON THE CLASSIC, THIS INTRODUCES THE UNIQUE DEPTH AND
FLAVOURS OF GALLIANO L'AUTENTICO.

serves 1

45 ml (1½ fl oz) dark rum
30 ml (1 fl oz) gold rum
2 teaspoons Galliano
3 teaspoons coconut cream

40 ml (1¼ fl oz) freshly squeezed
orange juice
30 ml (1 fl oz) pineapple juice,
fresh if possible
pineapple wedge, for garnish

Place the ingredients (except the garnish) in a high-speed blender with
1 cup ice and blend at high speed until smooth.

Pour into a poco grande glass and garnish with a pineapple wedge.

VOODOO

THIS VOODOO LADY WILL DRIVE YOU CRAZY.

serves 1

30 ml (1 fl oz) dark rum
30 ml (1 fl oz) aged rum
30 ml (1 fl oz) white rum
2 teaspoons smoky single
   malt whisky
60 ml (2 fl oz/¼ cup) pineapple
   juice, fresh if possible

60 ml (2 fl oz/¼ cup) freshly
   squeezed orange juice
pineapple wedge and maraschino
   cherry, for garnish

Place the ingredients (except the garnish) in a high-speed blender with 1 cup crushed ice. Blend at high speed for 5 seconds.

Pour into a tall glass and top with crushed ice. Garnish with a pineapple wedge and a maraschino cherry.

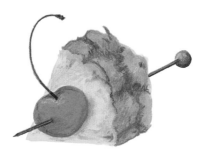

ACAPULCO

AH, MEMORIES OF MY TIME IN ACAPULCO: LOUNGING ON BEAUTIFUL BEACHES, SIPPING COCKTAILS, FRESH MEXICAN FOOD, MEMBERS OF THE LOCAL DRUG CARTEL EXECUTING PEOPLE WHILE RIDING JET SKIS … OH, AND THIS DRINK.

serves 1

45 ml (1½ fl oz) white rum
45 ml (1½ fl oz) orange curaçao
2 teaspoons freshly squeezed lime juice

2 teaspoons Sugar syrup (page 250)
1 egg white
mint sprig, for garnish

Combine the ingredients (except the garnish) in a cocktail shaker filled with ice. Shake.

Strain into an old fashioned glass filled with ice. Garnish with mint.

THE OTHER GUYS

Some people think they don't like rum. Those people are incorrect, but that's okay – in my experience, most of the world is incorrect. This doesn't mean they can't come to your fabulous tiki party. There are plenty of spirits that have risen from the mystical tiki ashes to flavour our fantastical cocktails.

Gin, vodka, tequila, whisky, brandy and bourbon are all drinks that should be drunk. After all, what is a drink without someone to drink it? They all have different flavours and characteristics that can add wonderfully subtle variations to the classic drinks we know and love.

This chapter is full of fun, fruity cocktails to drink when you're not drinking rum. So, it's time to raid your parents' liquor cabinet, fire up the blender and get this party started.

FROZEN MARGARITA

WHEN YOU WANT TO GIVE YOURSELF A HEADACHE BEFORE YOU GET A
HANGOVER, KNOCK BACK A COUPLE OF THESE IN QUICK SUCCESSION.

serves 1

60 ml (2 fl oz/¼ cup) tequila
3 teaspoons Cointreau
20 ml (¾ fl oz) freshly squeezed
  lime juice

20 ml (¾ fl oz) freshly squeezed
  lemon juice
3 teaspoons Sugar syrup
  (page 250)
salt and lime wheel, for garnish

Place the ingredients (except the garnish) in a high-speed blender with
1 cup ice. Blend at high speed until smooth.

Pour into a chilled cocktail glass rimmed with salt.

Garnish with a lime wheel.

MARGARITA

Nothing says party time like tequila. The margarita is all about balance of flavour: not too salty, not too sour and not too sweet. This is a drink worth perfecting.

serves 1

45 ml (1½ fl oz) tequila
3 teaspoons Cointreau
30 ml (1 fl oz) freshly squeezed
   lime juice

1½ teaspoons Sugar syrup
   (page 250)
salt and lime wedge, for garnish

Combine the ingredients (except the garnish) in a cocktail shaker filled with ice. Shake.

Strain into a chilled cocktail glass rimmed with salt.

Garnish with a lime wedge.

EL BURRO MARGARITA

This little donkey has two kicks. One from the tequila and another from the chilli.

Serves 1

80 g (2¾ oz/½ cup) chopped pineapple
3 sprigs coriander (cilantro)
45 ml (1½ fl oz) tequila
3 teaspoons Cointreau
30 ml (1 fl oz) freshly squeezed lime juice

3 teaspoons Sugar syrup (page 250)
2 dashes hot sauce
salt, lime wedge and chilli powder, for garnish

Muddle the pineapple and coriander in a cocktail shaker. Add the remaining ingredients (except the garnish) and fill the shaker with ice. Shake vigorously.

Strain into a chilled cocktail glass rimmed with salt.

Garnish with a lime wedge and a sprinkle of chilli powder.

PASSIONFRUIT MARGARITA

A SWEET AND ZESTY VERSION OF THE CLASSIC.

serves 1

45 ml (1½ fl oz) tequila
3 teaspoons Cointreau
pulp from 1 passionfruit (reserve
   ½ shell)
30 ml (1 fl oz) freshly squeezed
   lime juice

3 teaspoons Passionfruit syrup
   (page 256)
3 teaspoons green chartreuse

Combine the tequila, Cointreau, passionfruit pulp, lime juice and passionfruit syrup in a cocktail shaker filled with ice. Shake.

Strain into an old fashioned glass filled with ice.

Place the reserved passionfruit shell on top of the drink, pour in the chartreuse and carefully ignite.

WOODPECKER

This one will put some lead in your pencil.

Serves 1

60 ml (2 fl oz/¼ cup) cachaça
75 ml (2½ fl oz) freshly squeezed
  orange juice
3 teaspoons freshly squeezed
  lime juice

2 teaspoons Sugar syrup
  (page 250)
3 teaspoons Galliano
orange wheel and lime wedge,
  for garnish

Combine the cachaça, fruit juices and sugar syrup in a cocktail shaker filled with ice. Shake.

Strain into an old fashioned glass filled with crushed ice. Float the Galliano on top by pouring it over the back of a spoon.

Garnish with an orange wheel and a lime wedge.

SATURN

A GIN-BASED TIKI CHAMPION FROM BARTENDER J. 'POPO' GALSINI, CIRCA 1967.

Serves 1

45 ml (1½ fl oz) gin
3 teaspoons lemon juice
1 teaspoon Passionfruit syrup
   (page 256)
1 teaspoon Orgeat syrup
   (page 252)

1 teaspoon Velvet falernum
   (page 257)
mint sprig and lemon wheel,
   for garnish

Place the ingredients (except the garnish) in a high-speed blender with 1 cup ice. Blend at high speed for 5 seconds.

Pour into a tall glass and garnish with mint and a lemon wheel.

LAKA'S NECTAR

Laka is the Hawaiian goddess of dance. This homage to hula is from San Franciscan bartender Susan Eggett.

Serves 1

45 ml (1½ fl oz) silver mezcal
3 teaspoons white rum
3 teaspoons agave nectar

60 ml (2 fl oz/¼ cup) ginger beer
hibiscus flower, for garnish

Combine the mezcal, rum and agave nectar in a cocktail shaker filled with ice. Shake.

Strain into a tall glass filled with ice. Top with ginger beer and garnish with a hibiscus flower.

GONE NATIVE

I'M NOT SURE THERE'S A PLACE WHERE PIMM'S, GIN, APPLE AND GUAVA ARE ALL NATIVE, BUT I'D HAPPILY MOVE THERE IN A HEARTBEAT.

serves 1

45 ml (1½ fl oz) gin
3 teaspoons Pimm's No 1
30 ml (1 fl oz) guava juice
3 teaspoons freshly squeezed
  lemon juice

30 ml (1 fl oz) cloudy apple juice
mint sprig and guava slices, for
  garnish

Combine the ingredients (except the garnish) in a cocktail shaker filled with ice. Shake.

Strain into a tall glass filled with ice and garnish with mint and guava slices.

PiNEAPPLE NEGRONi

A SERIOUSLY SOPHISTICATED SIPPER THAT TIPS ITS TRILBY TO TIKI.

serves 1

30 ml (1 fl oz) pineapple rum
30 ml (1 fl oz) Campari

30 ml (1 fl oz) sweet vermouth
pineapple wedge, for garnish

Combine the ingredients (except the garnish) in an old fashioned glass filled with ice. Stir.

Garnish with a pineapple wedge.

TROTSKY

DRINK TOO MANY OF THESE AND YOU'LL FEEL IT LIKE A BLOW TO THE BACK
OF YOUR HEAD.

serves 2

60 ml (2 fl oz/¼ cup) Russian vodka
20 ml (¾ fl oz) freshly squeezed
  lemon juice
20 ml (¾ fl oz) Honey syrup

120 ml (4 fl oz) Russian caravan
  tea, chilled
lemon slices, for garnish

Combine the ingredients (except the garnish) in a teapot filled with ice
and stir.

Serve in tea cups with a wedge of lemon.

AGENT ORANGE

This drink contains so much booze it'll make your hair fall out.

serves 1

3 teaspoons tequila
3 teaspoons vodka
3 teaspoons dark rum
3 teaspoons white rum
3 teaspoons orange curaçao

60 ml (2 fl oz/¼ cup) freshly
   squeezed orange juice
2 teaspoons green chartreuse

Combine the ingredients (except the chartreuse) in a cocktail shaker filled with ice. Shake.

Strain into a tall glass filled with ice.

Float the chartreuse on top by pouring it over the back of a spoon and carefully igniting it.

HO'OPONOPONO POTION

An extremely drunk person once walked up to my bar and pointed to this cocktail on the menu. I said 'If you can say it, you can have it.' After four attempts he said, 'F#*k it,' and walked out.

Serves 1

4 slices cucumber, plus extra
  for garnish
45 ml (1½ fl oz) silver tequila
3 teaspoons Aperol

30 ml (1 fl oz) freshly squeezed
  lime juice
20 ml (¾ fl oz) Sugar syrup
  (page 250)

Muddle the cucumber slices (except the garnish) in a cocktail shaker. Add the other ingredients and fill the shaker with ice. Shake vigorously.

Strain into an old fashioned glass and add a large ice cube.

Garnish with a cucumber slice.

MEXICAN HEADHUNTER

HONEY, GINGER, SAGE AND TEQUILA MAKES FOR A VERY SEXY DRINK.

serves 1

3 sage leaves
30 ml (1 fl oz) reposado tequila
30 ml (1 fl oz) añejo tequila
1 teaspoon ginger liqueur
20 ml (¾ fl oz) freshly squeezed
lemon juice
3 teaspoons Sugar syrup
(page 250)

3 teaspoons Honey syrup
(page 253)
2 dashes Orange bitters (page 258)
mint and pineapple wedge, for
garnish

Lightly muddle the sage leaves in a cocktail shaker. Add the remaining ingredients (except the garnish) and fill the shaker with ice. Shake vigorously.

Pour the contents of the shaker into a tall glass. Garnish with mint and a pineapple wedge.

LONG ISLAND ICED TEA

This drink is an absolute classic. The recipe reads like some teenage kid has just raided their parents' liquor cabinet. Somehow, though, it works.

serves 1

3 teaspoons gin
3 teaspoons vodka
3 teaspoons white rum
3 teaspoons silver tequila
3 teaspoons Cointreau

30 ml (1 fl oz) freshly squeezed lemon juice
30 ml (1 fl oz) cola
lemon wheel, for garnish

Combine the liquor and lemon juice in a cocktail shaker filled with ice. Shake.

Strain into a large glass filled with ice and top with the cola.

Garnish with a lemon wheel.

HONi HONi

ONE OF TRADER VIC'S NON RUM-BASED TIKI CLASSICS, FOR ALL THE HONIS OUT THERE.

serves 1

60 ml (2 fl oz/¼ cup) bourbon
3 teaspoons orange curaçao
30 ml (1 fl oz) freshly squeezed lime juice

3 teaspoons Orgeat syrup (page 252)
maraschino cherry and pineapple wedge, for garnish

Combine the ingredients (except the garnish) in a cocktail shaker filled with ice. Shake.

Strain into an old fashioned glass filled with crushed ice. Garnish with a maraschino cherry and a pineapple wedge.

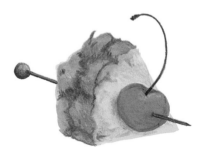

SUFFERiNG BASTARD

THIS DRINK COMES FROM THE SHEPHEARD'S HOTEL IN CAIRO AND DATES BACK TO WWII WHEN LIQUOR WAS IN SHORT SUPPLY. THEY BORROWED GIN FROM THE POSTAL EXCHANGE, BRANDY FROM CYPRUS AND BITTERS FROM THE CHEMIST ACROSS THE ROAD. NECESSITY REALLY IS THE MOTHER OF INVENTION.

serves 1

30 ml (1 fl oz) brandy or cognac
30 ml (1 fl oz) gin
3 teaspoons ginger liqueur
3 teaspoons freshly squeezed
  lime juice

60 ml (2 fl oz/¼ cup) ginger beer
3 dashes Orange bitters (page 258)
lime wedge, for garnish

Combine the liquor and lime juice in a cocktail shaker filled it with ice. Shake.

Strain into a tall glass filled with crushed ice and top with ginger beer.

Add the bitters and garnish with a lime wedge.

Chi Chi

The piña colada of the vodka world. Doesn't sound as good in the song though.

serves 1

60 ml (2 fl oz/¼ cup) vodka

100 ml (3½ fl oz) pineapple juice, fresh if possible

20 ml (¾ fl oz) coconut cream

3 teaspoons Sugar syrup (page 250)

3 teaspoons Orgeat syrup (page 252)

pineapple wedge and cocktail umbrella, for garnish

Place the ingredients (except the garnish) in a high-speed blender with 1½ cups crushed ice. Blend until smooth.

Pour into a poco grande glass and garnish with a pineapple wedge and cocktail umbrella.

SINGAPORE SLING

Here's a classic cocktail that actually comes from the place that it's named after. It was created by a Hainanese bartender called Ngiam Tong Boon, circa 1915.

Serves 1

30 ml (1 fl oz) gin
30 ml (1 fl oz) cherry brandy
30 ml (1 fl oz) orange curaçao
30 ml (1 fl oz) freshly squeezed lime juice

60 ml (2 fl oz/¼ cup) soda water (seltzer)
2 dashes Orange bitters (page 258)
maraschino cherry, for garnish

Pour the gin, cherry brandy, curaçao and lime juice into a tall glass filled with ice cubes. Top with the soda.

Add the bitters and garnish with a maraschino cherry.

Tiki Cocktails

BOOZY BORA BORA

When you're lounging under a grass hut on pure white sand overlooking the South Pacific Ocean, life feels like it can't get any better. That is until the waiter arrives with this wonderful invention.

Serves 1

45 ml (1½ fl oz) gin
90 ml (3 fl oz) cloudy apple juice
3 teaspoons Passionfruit syrup
 (page 256)

3 teaspoons freshly squeezed
 lemon juice
1 dash Grenadine (page 251)
pineapple wedge, for garnish

Combine the ingredients (except the grenadine and garnish) in a cocktail shaker filled with ice. Shake.

Strain into a highball glass filled with ice. Add the grenadine and garnish with a pineapple wedge.

CAIPIRINHA

The national cocktail of Brazil and you can just tell those guys know how to have a good time. Smashed limes, sugar and booze. Easy.

serves 1

1 lime, cut into 12 pieces
1 tablespoon soft brown sugar

60 ml (2 fl oz/¼ cup) cachaça
lime wheel, for garnish

Muddle the lime and sugar in a cocktail shaker. Add the cachaça and fill the shaker with ice. Shake vigorously.

Pour the contents of the shaker into an old fashioned glass and garnish with a lime wheel.

iLLUSiON SHAKER

During the 1990s many people made out with each other on the dance-floor because of this drink. Unfortunately, the illusion doesn't last for long.

serves 1

30 ml (1 fl oz) melon liqueur
45 ml (1½ fl oz) vodka
3 teaspoons coconut rum

3 teaspoons triple sec
45 ml (1½ fl oz) pineapple juice,
    fresh if possible

Combine the ingredients in a cocktail shaker filled with ice. Shake.

Stagger around a nightclub, staring into strangers' shot glasses.

The Other Guys

MINT JULEP

THIS CLASSIC DRINK OF THE KENTUCKY DERBY MAKES IT VERY RESPECTABLE TO DRINK BOURBON ON A HOT SUNNY DAY.

Serves 1

4 mint leaves
3 teaspoons mint syrup

60 ml (2 fl oz/¼ cup) bourbon
mint sprigs, for garnish

Muddle the mint leaves in a metal cup. Add the syrup and bourbon and stir to combine.

Fill the cup with crushed ice and garnish with fresh mint.

COSMOPOLITAN

PROBABLY THE MOST ORDERED COCKTAIL OF THE EARLY 21ST CENTURY, THIS DRINK IS GOOD FOR YOU AS CRANBERRY JUICE CONTAINS A LOT OF ANTIOXIDANTS AND VITAMIN C. THAT'S WHAT I TELL MY DOCTOR ANYWAY.

serves 1

30 ml (1 fl oz) vodka
30 ml (1 fl oz) Cointreau or
 triple sec
30 ml (1 fl oz) cranberry juice

3 teaspoons freshly squeezed
 lime juice
lemon, lime or orange twist,
 for garnish

Combine the ingredients (except the garnish) in a cocktail shaker filled with ice. Shake.

Strain into a chilled cocktail glass and garnish with a twist.

SEX ON THE BEACH

Sounds good, rarely is.

serves 1

45 ml (1½ fl oz) vodka
3 teaspoons peach schnapps
60 ml (2 fl oz/¼ cup) cranberry
    juice

60 ml (2 fl oz/¼ cup) freshly
    squeezed orange juice
cocktail umbrella, for garnish

Combine the ingredients (except the garnish) in a cocktail shaker filled with ice. Shake.

Strain into a tall glass filled with ice. Garnish with a cocktail umbrella.

WHISKY SOUR

A VERY SIMPLE DRINK, BUT A GREAT ONE. A GOOD WHISKY SOUR ENCOMPASSES THE CHARACTER OF TIKI BECAUSE IT'S ALL ABOUT TASTING THE FLAVOUR OF THE SPIRIT YOU PUT IN IT. TRY WITH DIFFERENT WHISKIES AND YOU'LL HAVE A COMPLETELY DIFFERENT EXPERIENCE EACH TIME. THIS DRINK USES RAW EGG WHITE TO GIVE IT A FLUFFY FOAM. IF YOU'RE PREGNANT, OMIT THE EGG WHITE ... AND THE WHISKY.

serves 1

60 ml (2 fl oz/¼ cup) whisky
40 ml (1¼ fl oz) freshly squeezed
  lemon juice
20 ml (¾ fl oz) Sugar syrup
  (page 250)

1 egg white
maraschino cherry, for garnish

Combine the ingredients (except the garnish) in a cocktail shaker filled with ice and shake vigorously.

Strain into an old fashioned glass filled with ice. Garnish with a maraschino cherry.

AMARETTO SOUR

A VARIATION ON THE WHISKY SOUR, THIS IS MADE WITH AMARETTO – AN ITALIAN ALMOND LIQUEUR. ONCE AGAIN, YOU CAN LEAVE OUT THE EGG WHITE IF YOU'RE VEGAN OR SOMETHING.

serves 1

60 ml (2 fl oz/¼ cup) amaretto
40 ml (1¼ fl oz) freshly squeezed
   lemon juice
20 ml (¾ fl oz) Orgeat syrup
   (page 252)

1 egg white
maraschino cherry, for garnish

Combine the ingredients (except the garnish) in a cocktail shaker filled with ice and shake vigorously.

Strain into an old fashioned glass filled with ice.

Garnish with a maraschino cherry.

BLUE LAGOON

This drink screams 70s cocktail party. Fire up the fondue, dial up the disco and bring on your best Brooke Shields impersonation

Serves 1

60 ml (2 fl oz/¼ cup) vodka
3 teaspoons blue curaçao

100 ml (3½ fl oz) lemonade
maraschino cherry, for garnish

Combine the vodka and curaçao in a tall glass filled with ice. Top with with lemonade.

Garnish with a maraschino cherry.

Pimm's Cup

Anyone for tennis? Rowing? Polo? Other equestrian events? This drink is as English as cucumber sandwiches and Devonshire tea, but it's delicious and fruity, so fits the tiki bill nicely.

serves 1

30 ml (1 fl oz) gin
45 ml (1½ fl oz) Pimm's No 1
slices of cucumber, apple, orange,
    lemon, lime

6 mint leaves
90 ml (3 fl oz) ginger ale

Combine the ingredients in a tall glass filled with ice and stir.

PINK LADY

Slender and stylish with a twist.

serves 1

60 ml (2 fl oz/¼ cup) gin

3 teaspoons triple sec

30 ml (1 fl oz) freshly squeezed lemon juice

1½ teaspoons Grenadine (page 251)

lemon twist, for garnish

Combine the ingredients (except the garnish) in a cocktail shaker filled with ice. Shake.

Strain into a chilled cocktail glass. Garnish with a lemon twist.

SHIRLEY TEMPLE, ALL GROWN UP

ONCE A SWEET LITTLE INNOCENT CHILD, NOW A FULL-GROWN WOMAN WHO CAN PUT YOU ON YOUR BEHIND.

Serves 1

60 ml (2 fl oz/¼ cup) vodka
3 teaspoons freshly squeezed
lime juice
90 ml (3 fl oz) ginger beer

3 teaspoons Grenadine (page 251)
1 tablespoon passionfruit pulp
orange wheel, for garnish

Pour the vodka and lime juice into a highball glass filled with ice and top with the ginger beer. Stir.

Slowly add the grenadine, pouring against the inside of the glass so that it sinks to the bottom.

Spoon the passionfruit pulp on top and garnish with an orange wheel.

LA BAMBA

A LITTLE LIKE A COCONUT CHERRY CANDY BAR, THIS IS A DESSERT COCKTAIL MADE FOR COCONUT LOVERS.

serves 1

45 ml (1½ fl oz) cachaça
30 ml (1 fl oz) coconut rum
3 teaspoons maraschino cherry liqueur

3 teaspoons maraschino cherry juice
45 ml (1½ fl oz) cream
maraschino cherry, for garnish

Combine the ingredients (except the garnish) in a cocktail shaker filled with ice. Shake.

Strain into a chilled cocktail glass and garnish with a maraschino cherry.

SALTY SEA DOG

WHEN YOU FINALLY REACH THE PORT AFTER MANY NIGHTS ON THE STORMY SEAS, YOU REALLY NEED A SOPHISTICATED PINK DRINK TO WHET YOUR WHISTLE.

Serves 1

30 ml (1 fl oz) tequila
3 teaspoons Campari
60 ml (2 fl oz/¼ cup) freshly
squeezed pink grapefruit juice

pink grapefruit slice and cocktail
umbrella, for garnish

Combine the ingredients (except the garnish) in an old fashioned glass rimmed with salt and filled with ice.

Garnish with a pink grapefruit slice and a cocktail umbrella.

CARIBBEAN SUNRISE

The brother-from-another-mother to the Tequila Sunrise. This one moves closer to its tiki roots.

Serves 1

60 ml (2 fl oz/¼ cup) Caribbean rum

90 ml (3 fl oz) freshly squeezed orange juice

3 teaspoons Grenadine (page 251)

pineapple wedge, for garnish

Combine the rum and orange juice in a tall glass filled with ice.

Slowly add the grenadine, pouring against the inside of the glass so that it sinks to the bottom.

Garnish with a pineapple wedge.

PEACH & GINGER COBBLER

WHO DOESN'T LOVE PEACH COBBLER? THE ONLY WAY TO IMPROVE ON IT IS TO MAKE IT INTO AN ALCOHOLIC BEVERAGE AND SET IT ON FIRE.

serves 1

60 ml (2 fl oz/¼ cup) rye whiskey

2 teaspoons ginger liqueur

60 ml (2 fl oz/¼ cup) peach nectar

3 teaspoons Orgeat syrup (page 252)

1 dash Orange bitters (page 258)

4 fresh mint leaves, chopped

3 teaspoons freshly squeezed lemon juice.

½ peach, stone removed

1 teaspoon soft brown sugar

2 teaspoons 151 proof rum

Combine the whiskey, ginger liqueur, peach nectar, orgeat syrup, bitters, mint and lemon juice in a cocktail shaker filled with ice. Shake.

Strain into a large old fashioned glass filled with ice.

Place the peach in the top of the drink, cut side up. Fill the cavity with the sugar and rum and carefully ignite.

RASBERRY GIN RICKEY

The essence of tiki cocktails is fresh fruit that's in season. There are few things better than fresh raspberries. In fact, the only thing better is fresh raspberries floating in gin.

serves 4

375 g (13 oz/3 cups) fresh
  raspberries, plus extra
  for garnish
110 g (4 oz/½ cup) sugar
120 ml (4 fl oz) freshly squeezed
  lime juice

250 ml (8½ fl oz/1 cup) gin
soda water (seltzer), for topping
lime wedges, for garnish

Place the raspberries, sugar and lime juice in a small jug and muddle gently. Add the gin and leave to steep at room temperature for 2–3 hours, stirring occasionally.

When ready to serve, pour into old fashioned glasses filled with ice and top with soda.

Garnish with fresh raspberries and lime wedges.

APEROL SPRITZER

This is more of a sophisticated drink than the classic tiki concoctions. However, it is bright red and uses a liqueur made from rhubarb among other ingredients, so I feel like it would fit right in at the tiki family Christmas.

Serves 1

30 ml (1 fl oz) gin
30 ml (1 fl oz) Aperol
60 ml (2 fl oz/¼ cup) sparkling wine
   or soda water (seltzer)

orange wheel and green olives,
   for garnish

Combine the gin and Aperol in a large wine glass and fill with ice.

Top with sparkling wine or soda water, depending on how boozy you want to get.

Garnish with an orange wheel and olives.

Tiki Cocktails

TEQUILA SUNRISE

This little tiki number came fairly late in the piece – circa 1970s – and was favoured by Mick Jagger. He had a kid at the age of 72. Must have been all that vitamin C.

Serves 1

60 ml (2 fl oz/¼ cup) tequila
90 ml (3 fl oz) freshly squeezed
  orange juice

3 teaspoons Grenadine
  (page 251)
maraschino cherry, for garnish

Combine the tequila and orange juice in a tall glass filled with ice.

Slowly add the grenadine, pouring against the inside of the glass so that it sinks to the bottom.

Garnish with a maraschino cherry and continue on your rock and roll tour.

PISCO IN THE SNOW

THE BEST YELLOW SNOW YOU'LL HAVE ALL DAY.

serves 1

30 ml (1 fl oz) white rum
3 teaspoons lemon juice
20 ml (¾ fl oz) Passionfruit syrup
(page 256)

30 ml (1 fl oz) pisco brandy
lemon twist, for garnish

Combine the rum, lemon juice and passionfruit syrup in a cocktail shaker filled with ice. Shake.

Strain into an old fashioned glass and fill with crushed ice.

Pour pisco brandy into the centre of the ice and garnish with a lemon twist.

CACTUS COLADA

¿TE GUSTA PIÑAS COLADAS Y QUEDAR ATRAPADO EN LA LLUVIA?

serves 1

60 ml (2 fl oz/¼ cup) tequila

3 teaspoons coconut rum

2 teaspoons Orgeat syrup (page 252)

30 ml (1 fl oz) pineapple juice, fresh if possible

30 ml (1 fl oz) freshly squeezed orange juice

2 teaspoons Grenadine (page 251)

20 ml (¾ fl oz) coconut cream

opened coconut, for serving (optional)

Place the ingredients (except the coconut) in a high-speed blender filled with ice. Blend at high speed until smooth.

Pour into a coconut (or a large cocktail glass) and top with crushed ice.

PiNE—LiME SPLiCE

This drink screams summer. Tropical fruit, coconut rum; plus it's green and it tastes like a popsicle.

serves 1

30 ml (1 fl oz) vodka
30 ml (1 fl oz) coconut rum
30 ml (1 fl oz) melon liqueur
90 ml (3 fl oz) pineapple juice, fresh if possible

30 ml (1 fl oz) cream
pineapple wedge and pineapple leaves, to garnish

Combine the vodka, rum and liqueur in a poco grande glass filled with ice. Top with pineapple juice, ensuring that there's some room left at the top.

Float the cream on top by pouring it over the back of a spoon.

Garnish with a pineapple wedge and pineapple leaves.

BITTER AND TWISTED

Blood orange is definitely the coolest of all the oranges. When you cut it, it bleeds. They're not available all year round, so take advantage of them when they're in season.

serves 1

30 ml (1 fl oz) gin
30 ml (1 fl oz) Campari
30 ml (1 fl oz) red vermouth

60 ml (2 fl oz/¼ cup) freshly squeezed blood orange juice
blood orange twist, for garnish

Combine the ingredients (except the garnish) in an old fashioned glass filled with ice.

Garnish with a blood orange twist.

THE BEE KEEPER

Honey and lemon have been hanging out together since the dawn of culinary time.

serves 1

45 ml (1½ fl oz) cognac
30 ml (1 fl oz) orange curaçao
30 ml (1 fl oz) freshly squeezed lemon juice

3 teaspoons Honey syrup (page 253)
lemon wheel, for garnish

Combine the ingredients (except the garnish) in a cocktail shaker filled with ice. Shake.

Strain into a chilled cocktail glass and garnish with a lemon wheel.

BLOODY GOOD BLOODY MARY

THIS BLOODY WONDERFUL DRINK IS BEST SERVED AT BREAKFAST TIME WITH ALL OF THE CONDIMENTS ON THE SIDE SO YOU CAN ADJUST THE FLAVOUR TO YOUR LIKING. ALSO, YOU CAN GARNISH YOUR MARY WITH WHATEVER YOU FEEL LIKE.

Serves 1

45 ml (1½ fl oz) vodka

2 teaspoons dry sherry

2 teaspoons rich red wine

25 ml (¾ fl oz) freshly squeezed lemon juice

generous few dashes hot sauce

pinch of celery salt

freshly ground black pepper

90 ml (3 fl oz) good-quality tomato juice

pickled chilli, gherkin (pickle), barbecued prawn (shrimp) and celery stalk, for garnish

Combine the vodka, sherry, wine, lemon juice, hot sauce, celery salt and pepper in a large glass. Stir. Fill with ice and top with the tomato juice.

Check the flavour and adjust to taste.

Thread a chilli, gherkin and prawn onto a long skewer and place into the drink along with a celery stalk.

TIGER LILLET

Lillet is a French wine-based aperitif that should be more popular. Great to drink on a hot summer's day. Vive le distillation.

serves 1

60 ml (2 fl oz/¼ cup) Lillet Blanc
30 ml (1 fl oz) Campari

30 ml (1 fl oz) freshly squeezed
    pink grapefruit juice
blood orange twist, for garnish

Combine the ingredients (except the garnish) in an old fashioned glass filled with ice.

Garnish with a blood orange twist.

MiNT SPRiG

Fresh mint, cucumber and gin make for a refreshing afternoon tipple.

serves 1

60 ml (2 fl oz/¼ cup) cucumber gin

30 ml (1 fl oz) freshly squeezed
lime juice

20 ml (¾ fl oz) Grenadine
(page 251)

3 teaspoons Sugar syrup
(page 250)

90 ml (3 fl oz) soda water (seltzer)

mint sprig and cucumber ribbon,
to garnish

Combine the ingredients (except the garnish) in a tall glass filled with crushed ice and stir to combine.

Garnish with mint and a cucumber ribbon.

MONKEY WRENCH

BECAUSE YOU SHOULD HAVE MORE THAN JUST SCREWDRIVERS IN YOUR TOOL BOX.

Serves 1

30 ml (1 fl oz) vodka

3 teaspoons coconut rum

60 ml (2 fl oz/¼ cup) pineapple juice, fresh if possible

60 ml (2 fl oz/¼ cup) freshly squeezed orange juice

orange slice and plastic monkey, for garnish

Combine the ingredients (except the garnish) in a cocktail shaker filled with ice. Shake.

Strain into a tall glass filled with ice.

Garnish with an orange wheel and one of those little plastic monkeys they used to put on drinks in the 1980s.

GiNGER MEGGS

A LITTLE RASCAL OF A DRINK WITH THE WARMTH OF GINGER AND THE ACIDITY OF LEMON JUICE, PERFECTLY BALANCED WITH SWEET CINNAMON AND PINEAPPLE.

Serves 1

45 ml (1½ fl oz) vodka

3 teaspoons ginger liqueur

30 ml (1 fl oz) freshly squeezed lemon juice

30 ml (1 fl oz) pineapple juice, fresh if possible

3 teaspoons Cinnamon syrup (page 255)

pineapple wedge and star anise, for garnish

Combine the ingredients (except the garnish) in a cocktail shaker filled with ice. Shake.

Strain into a tall glass filled with crushed ice. Garnish with a pineapple wedge and star anise.

SMOKE STACK

THE FLAVOURS IN THIS DRINK DEVELOP AS YOU MAKE YOUR WAY
TO THE BOTTOM.

SERVES 1

30 ml (1 fl oz) Irish whiskey

3 teaspoons ginger liqueur

30 ml (1 fl oz) freshly squeezed
lemon juice

20 ml (¾ fl oz) Sugar syrup
(page 250)

20 ml (¾ fl oz) Honey syrup
(page 253)

60 ml (2 fl oz/¼ cup) soda water
(seltzer)

3 teaspoons smoky single malt
whisky

Place the Irish whiskey, liqueur, lemon juice and syrups in a high-speed
blender with 1 cup crushed ice. Blend at high speed for 5 seconds.

Pour into a tall glass and top with crushed ice and soda.

Float the single malt on top by pouring it over the back of a spoon.

FROZEN BikiNi

WHEN YOU SPIKE A BELLINI AND CHILL IT, YOU GET A FROZEN BIKINI.

Serves 1

30 ml (1 fl oz) vodka
3 teaspoons peach schnapps
30 ml (1 fl oz) peach nectar

90 ml (3 fl oz) sparkling white wine
strawberry, for garnish

Place the vodka, schnapps and nectar in a high-speed blender with 1 cup ice and blend at high speed until smooth.

Pour into a chilled champagne flute and top with sparkling wine.

Garnish with a strawberry.

HONOLULU

This hot Hawaiian honey will have your heart heaving.

serves 1

60 ml (2 fl oz/¼ cup) gin

3 teaspoons pineapple juice,
fresh if possible

2 teaspoons freshly squeezed
lemon juice

2 dashes Orange bitters (page 258)

sugar and lemon wheel, for garnish

Combine the ingredients (except the garnish) in a cocktail shaker filled
with ice. Shake.

Strain into a chilled cocktail glass rimmed with sugar. Garnish with
a lemon wheel.

FRUIT TINGLE

THIS MODERN TIKI COCKTAIL WAS A GATEWAY DRINK FOR MANY YOUNG PEOPLE IN THE LATE 20TH CENTURY. EVERYONE LIKES SOMETHING SWEET AND BLUE IN THEIR MOUTH.

serves 1

45 ml (1½ fl oz) vodka
3 teaspoons blue curaçao
100 ml (3½ fl oz) lemonade

3 teaspoons Grenadine
(page 251)
fresh cherry, for garnish

Pour the vodka and blue curaçao into a hurricane glass filled with ice and top with the lemonade. Stir.

Slowly add the grenadine, pouring against the inside of the glass so that it sinks to the bottom.

Garnish with a cherry and your old fake ID.

PUNCH BOWLS

Nothing gets a party started like a punch. I'm not talking about an 'outside a nightclub at four in the morning' kind of punch, I'm talking about a big ol' bowl full of fruit, juice, huge elaborate garnishes and a metric shirt-load of booze.

These recipes can be for four or forty, depending on how good at drinking you and your friends are. Almost anything can be used as a punchbowl. From ornate ceramic tiki bowls with a flaming volcano in the middle to fish bowls, buckets, beautiful (or hideous) giant glass salad bowls, basins, baths, basically whatever you can find to hold many gallons of wonderful punch.

Get creative and make your punchbowl the centrepiece of your party.

SCORPION BOWL

THIS IS A CLASSIC TIKI PUNCH FROM THE MASTER HIMSELF, DONN BEACH. IT HAS ITS OWN SIGNATURE SERVING BOWL WITH A VOLCANO-SHAPED CUP IN THE CENTRE. THIS CUP IS FILLED WITH OVER-PROOFED RUM AND SET ALIGHT.

Serves 5–10

300 ml (10 fl oz) dark rum

60 ml (2 fl oz/¼ cup) brandy or cognac

90 ml (3 fl oz) Orgeat syrup (page 252)

125 ml (4 fl oz/½ cup) freshly squeezed lemon juice

90 ml (3 fl oz) freshly squeezed orange juice

90 ml (3 fl oz) pineapple juice, fresh if possible

90 ml (3 fl oz) guava juice

cinnamon sticks, edible flowers, and lime slices, for garnish

squeezed lime half

3 teaspoons 151 proof rum

Place the ingredients (except the garnish, lime half and 151 proof rum) in a high-speed blender with ½ cup crushed ice. Blend until smooth.

Pour into a scorpion bowl or large punch bowl and add blocks of ice. Garnish with cinnamon sticks, edible flowers and lime slices.

Invert the lime half so that the skin side creates a cup. Place it in the centre of the scorpion bowl or float it in the punch. Fill the lime cup with 151 proof rum and carefully ignite.

PLANTER'S PUNCH

This spicy and delicious classic comes from the Planters Inn in South Carolina. Humphrey Bogart orders a Planters Punch in the film *Across the Pacific*.

serves 5–10

150 ml (5 fl oz) dark rum
150 ml (5 fl oz) white rum
90 ml (3 fl oz) orange curaçao
185 ml (6 fl oz/¾ cup) freshly
    squeezed orange juice
90 ml (3 fl oz) freshly squeezed
    lime juice
90 ml (3 fl oz) Sugar syrup
    (page 250)

3 teaspoons Allspice dram
    (page 259)
90 ml (3 fl oz) Grenadine
    (page 251)
1 tablespoon Orange bitters
    (page 258)
pineapple pieces, orange
    and lime wheels, for garnish

Combine the ingredients (except the garnish) in a large punch bowl with large blocks of ice. Chill for 2–4 hours.

Add more ice and garnish with pineapple pieces and orange and lime wheels.

HURRiCANE PUNCH

THIS IS A LARGER VERSION OF THE 1940S CLASSIC COCKTAIL FROM NEW
ORLEANS. FRUITY, NUTTY AND SWEET, HURRICANE PUNCH IS PERFECT FOR
A SUNNY AFTERNOON WITH FRIENDS. OR A GLOOMY AFTERNOON ALONE.

serves 10

350 ml (12 fl oz) dark rum
350 ml (12 fl oz) white rum
300 ml (10 fl oz) freshly squeezed
orange juice
300 ml (10 fl oz) pineapple juice,
fresh if possible
300 ml (10 fl oz) freshly squeezed
lime juice

150 ml (5 fl oz) passionfruit juice
30 ml (1 fl oz) Orgeat syrup
(page 252)
30 ml (1 fl oz) Grenadine
(page 251)
orange wheels and maraschino
cherries, for garnish

Combine the ingredients (except the garnish) in a large punch bowl
with large blocks of ice. Chill for 2–4 hours.

Add more ice and garnish with orange wheels and maraschino cherries.

TAHITIAN RUM PUNCH

This was one of Donn Beach's first cocktails, dating back to 1934. It's full of fruit and rum so it's a great drink if you're at risk of getting scurvy.

Serves 10–20

500 g (1 lb 2 oz) soft brown sugar

1 litre (34 fl oz/4 cups) white rum

750 ml (25½ fl oz/3 cups) dark rum

700 ml (23½ fl oz) dry white or sparkling wine

1 litre (34 fl oz/4 cups) freshly squeezed orange juice

1 litre (34 fl oz/4 cups) freshly squeezed grapefruit juice

1 litre (34 fl oz/4 cups) pineapple juice, fresh if possible

500 ml (17 fl oz/2 cups) freshly squeezed lime juice

60 ml (2 fl oz/¼ cup) Vanilla syrup (page 254)

3 bananas, sliced

6 oranges, cut into slices

3 grapefruit, cut into slices

1 pineapple, cored and cut into chunks

pineapple leaves, star fruit and maraschino cherries, for garnish

Combine the sugar with 250 ml (8½ fl oz/1 cup) water in a large saucepan over medium–high heat, stirring until the sugar is dissolved. Set aside to cool.

In a very large punch bowl, combine the brown sugar syrup with the rest of the ingredients and large blocks of ice. Allow to chill overnight.

Garnish with pineapple leaves, star fruit and maraschino cherries.

VOODOO JUiCE

Drink too much of this and you may find yourself dancing around an open fire with your shirt off and speaking in tongues.

serves 20–30

700 ml (23½ fl oz) coconut rum
700 ml (23½ fl oz) banana rum
700 ml (23½ fl oz) pineapple rum
700 ml (23½ fl oz) orange rum
700 ml (23½ fl oz) spiced rum
2 litres (68 fl oz/8 cups) cranberry juice

2 litres (68 fl oz/8 cups) freshly squeezed orange juice
2 litres (68 fl oz/8 cups), pineapple juice, fresh if possible
pineapple pieces and orange, banana, lemon and lime slices, for garnish

Combine the ingredients in a very large punch bowl along with large blocks of ice.

Allow to chill overnight.

TONGA PUNCH

This is one of Trader Vic's classic recipes. Balanced acidity, lighter on the booze, pink and garnished with flowers. A very pretty drink indeed.

Serves 15–20

1 litre (34 fl oz/4 cups) white rum
300 ml (10 fl oz) orange curaçao
1 litre (34 fl oz/4 cups) freshly squeezed orange juice
500 ml (17 fl oz/2 cups) freshly squeezed lemon juice

150 ml (5 fl oz) freshly squeezed lime juice
100 ml (3½ fl oz) Grenadine (page 251)
edible flowers, for garnish

Combine the ingredients (except the garnish) in a large punch bowl with large blocks of ice. Chill for 2–4 hours.

Add more ice and garnish with edible flowers.

FiSH HOUSE PUNCH

The oldest recipe in this book, the first known record of Fish House Punch goes all the way back to 1744, in Philadelphia's fishing club, known as The Fish House. Allegedly, when George Washington drank this punchy iced tea he was unable to make a diary entry for the next three days.

serves 10–20

peeled rind of 4 lemons
220 g (8 oz/1 cup) sugar
500 ml (17 fl oz/2 cups) warm English breakfast tea
500 ml (17 fl oz/2 cups) warm earl grey tea
250 ml (8½ fl oz/1 cup) freshly squeezed lemon juice

1 litre (34 fl oz/4 cups) dark rum
500 ml (17 fl oz/2 cups) brandy or cognac
125 ml (4 fl oz/½ cup) peach brandy
lemon wheels and freshly grated nutmeg, for garnish

In a large punch bowl, rub the lemon rind and sugar together to release the oils from the rind. Allow to infuse for 1 hour.

Pour the teas into the bowl and stir until the sugar is dissolved. Add the lemon juice and liquor, and stir to combine.

Add a very large block of ice, then continue to add smaller blocks of ice to achieve the desired dilution.

Garnish with lemon wheels and nutmeg.

SANGRIA

EVERYONE SHOULD KNOW HOW TO MAKE A GOOD SANGRIA – THE ICONIC
DRINK OF SPAIN. THIS PUNCH IS A GREAT WAY TO USE UP SOME OF THOSE
BOTTLES OF CHEAP RED WINE PEOPLE KEEP GIVING YOU AT HOLIDAY TIME.

serves 5–10

2 x 750 ml (25½ fl oz/3 cups)
  bottles fruity red wine or sparkling
  shiraz
700 ml (23½ fl oz) sparkling white
  wine
500 ml (17 fl oz/2 cups) brandy
  or cognac
4 peaches, stones removed
  and sliced

2 lemons, sliced
3 oranges, sliced
3 limes, sliced
100 ml (3½ fl oz) Passionfruit syrup
  (page 256)
1.25 litres (42 fl oz/5 cups) soda
  water (seltzer)

Combine the ingredients (except the soda water) in a large punch bowl
with large blocks of ice. Chill for 4–6 hours.

When ready to serve, add soda water and more ice.

EUREKA PUNCH

SOMETIMES PUNCH IS WHAT YOU NEED TO REALLY GET A PARTY STARTED.
THE EUREKA IS PERFECT – IT'S REALLY BOOZY AND YOU CAN SET IT ON FIRE.
WHAT MORE COULD YOU WANT IN A PUNCH?

serves 30–40

1.5 litres (51 fl oz/6 cups) aged rum
600 ml (20½ fl oz) yellow chartreuse
1 litre (34 fl oz/4 cups) Honey syrup
(page 253)
1.5 litres (51 fl oz/6 cups) freshly
squeezed lemon juice

1½ tablespoons Orange bitters
(page 258)
2.5 litres (85 fl oz/10 cups) ginger ale
mint sprigs, lemon wheels and
edible flowers, for garnish

In a 5 litre (1.3 gallon) container, combine the rum, chartreuse, honey
syrup, lemon juice and bitters with large blocks of ice and 250 ml
(8½ fl oz/1 cup) iced water. Chill for at least 2 hours.

Serve into several punch bowls, or one enormous vessel. Top with
ginger ale, ice and garnish with mint, lemon wheels and edible flowers.

*This drink can be set on fire due to the large quantity of yellow chartreuse.
If you wish to do so, first ensure your punch is in a heatproof vessel. Light
a match then, using a long-handled metal spoon, pick up a spoonful of the
punch. Bring the spoon to the match to light, then carefully bring the lit spoon
to the punch bowl. Make sure you're standing back when it ignites, and use
a large saucepan lid or a frying pan to extinguish the flame.*

THE SEAWARD

The classic coconut and pineapple combination that screams "tropical holiday".

serves 6–12

1 litre (34 fl oz/4 cups) spiced rum

500 ml (17 fl oz/2 cups) Grand Marnier

500 ml (17 fl oz/2 cups) coconut rum

2 litres (68 fl oz/8 cups) pineapple juice, fresh if possible

500 ml (17 fl oz/2 cups) freshly squeezed orange juice

500 ml (17 fl oz/2 cups) coconut cream

pineapple wedge and shaved coconut, for garnish

Combine the liquor and juices in a large punch bowl with large blocks of ice. Chill for 2–4 hours.

When ready to serve, add more ice and top with coconut cream. Stir to combine.

Garnish with a pineapple wedge and shaved coconut.

FUN iN THE SHRUBBS

This recipe comes courtesy of Greg Amor from Rose Bar in Melbourne. I've had a couple of drinks with Greg – he knows what he's doing.

serves 6–12

1 litre (34 fl oz/4 cups) dark rum
500 ml (17 fl oz/2 cups) Creole Shrubb rum
500 ml (17 fl oz/2 cups) freshly squeezed lime juice

4 dashes Angostura Bitters
4 dashes Orange bitters (page 258)
300 ml (10 fl oz) Sugar syrup (page 250)
lime and orange wheels, for garnish

Combine the ingredients (except the garnish) in a large punch bowl with large blocks of ice. Chill for 2–4 hours.

When ready to serve, add more ice and garnish with lime and orange wheels.

WATERMELON MARGARITA

THIS IS A REAL CENTREPIECE FOR THE TABLE AS IT'S SERVED IN A WHOLE WATERMELON. NOTHING SAYS SUMMER LIKE WATERMELON, AND NOTHING SAYS PARTY TIME LIKE TEQUILA.

serves 6–12

1 whole chilled watermelon
700 ml (23½ fl oz) tequila
90 ml (3 fl oz) freshly squeezed
  lemon juice

90 ml (3 fl oz) Sugar syrup
  (page 250)
grapes, watermelon cubes and
  cocktail umbrella, to garnish

Cut a hole in the watermelon big enough to fit an electric egg beater or stick blender. Reserve some for garnish, then blitz the flesh of the watermelon.

Remove 1 litre (34 fl oz/4 cups) watermelon juice and set aside.

Add the tequila, lemon juice and sugar syrup. Stir to combine and top up with watermelon juice as required.

Chill until ready to serve. Garnish with grapes, watermelon cubes and a cocktail umbrella.

KOOKOO CACHAÇA

Cachaça is a fantastic spirit to use in cocktails. It's made from distilled sugar cane juice and hails from Brazil. Put it with any kind of fruit and you won't go far wrong.

serves 6

1 litre (34 fl oz/4 cups) cachaça
500 ml (17 fl oz/2 cups) pineapple vodka
500 ml (17 fl oz/2 cups) freshly squeezed lemon juice
500 ml (17 fl oz/2 cups) Grenadine (page 251)

1 litre (34 fl oz/4 cups) soda water (seltzer)
pineapple pieces and lemon wheels, for garnish

Combine the ingredients (except the soda water and garnish) in a large punch bowl with large blocks of ice. Chill for 2–4 hours.

When ready to serve, add more ice and top with soda. Garnish with pineapple pieces and lemon wheels.

COOK ISLAND CUCKOLD

Fruity, alcoholic and tart ... are words I use to describe my ex.
This drink is a great way to take your mind off things.

serves 10–15

1 litre (34 fl oz/4 cups) vodka
2 litres (68 fl oz/8 cups) pineapple
  juice
250 ml (8½ fl oz/1 cup) cranberry
  juice

700 ml (23½ fl oz) sparkling wine,
  chilled
pineapple pieces, strawberry
  halves and lemon wheels,
  for garnish

Combine the vodka and fruit juices in a large punch bowl with large
blocks of ice. Chill for 2–4 hours.

When ready to serve, top with the sparkling wine and more ice.

Garnish with the pineapple pieces, strawberries and lemon wheels.

PASSION PUNCH

FILL THE BOWL WITH THIS BABY AND INVITE EVERYONE IN FOR
A PASSION PARTY.

serves 10

1 litre (34 fl oz/4 cups) lemon vodka

500 ml (17 fl oz/2 cups) guava juice

700 ml (23½ fl oz) cloudy apple
juice

250 ml (8½ fl oz/1 cup) Passionfruit
syrup (page 256)

1 litre (34 fl oz/4 cups) dry cider

pineapple pieces and lime wheels,
for garnish.

Combine the vodka, fruit juices and syrup in a large punch bowl
with large blocks of ice. Chill for 2–4 hours.

When ready to serve, top with the cider and more ice.

Garnish with pineapple pieces and lime wheels.

PEACH MIMOSA

NOT SO MUCH A PUNCHBOWL, BUT IT IS A DRINK THAT SERVES 10. YOU CAN SPIKE IT WITH VODKA OR WHITE RUM IF YOU WANT MORE OF A PUNCH.

SERVES 8–10

500 ml (17 fl oz/2 cups) peach nectar

250 ml (8½ fl oz/1 cup) freshly squeezed orange juice

90 ml (3 fl oz) Grenadine (page 251)

700 ml (23½ fl oz) sparkling wine

Chill all of your ingredients and champagne flutes completely before starting.

In a small jug, combine the peach nectar, orange juice and grenadine. Stir to combine.

Evenly distribute among chilled champagne flutes and top with sparkling wine.

SYRUPS, BATTERS AND BITTERS

At Don the Beachcomber's, the original tiki bar, they made all of their own secret mixes of syrups, batters, bitters and spice mixes. The owner, Donn Beach, was so protective of his recipes, even the bartenders were kept in the dark as to what was in a lot of the mixers.

He had unlabelled bottles with things like 'Don's Spices #2' and 'Don's Mix' written on them, the contents of which was only known by Donn himself. Over the years, many bartenders have tried to work out what was in Donn's secret recipes but no one will ever truly know – Donn died in 1989, taking his knowledge with him.

You can spend a lot of money on pre-made cocktail ingredients, but in this chapter we have some basic tiki staples that will get you started.

SUGAR SYRUP

makes 500 ml (17 fl oz/2 cups)

440 g (15½ oz/2 cups) sugar

In a small saucepan, bring 500 ml (17 fl oz/2 cups) water to the boil. Add the sugar and stir until dissolved.

Remove from the heat and set aside to cool. Pour into a sterilized bottle or jar.

This sugar syrup will keep in the fridge for up to 1 month.

To make Demerara syrup, replace sugar with demerara sugar.

GRENADINE

makes 1 litre (34 fl oz/4 cups)

4 pomegranates, juiced (or 1 litre/
   34 fl oz/4 cups pomegranate juice)
440 g (15½ oz/2 cups) sugar

juice of 1 lemon
30 ml (1 fl oz) vodka (optional)

In a saucepan over medium–high heat, bring the pomegranate juice to the boil and simmer until reduced by half. Add the sugar and stir until dissolved, then add the lemon juice.

If you wish to store the grenadine for longer than 1 month, add the vodka (it acts as a preservative).

Remove from the heat and set aside to cool. Pour into a sterilized bottle or jar.

This grenadine will keep in the fridge for up to 1 month, or 3 months with vodka added.

ORGEAT SYRUP

makes 1 litre (34 fl oz/4 cups)

500 g (1 lb 2 oz) raw almonds,
    soaked in warm water for
    30 minutes

700 g (1 lb 9 oz) sugar
50 ml (1¾ fl oz) brandy

Drain the almonds and discard the water.

In a food processor, blend the almonds into a paste, adding a little water if needed. Transfer to a bowl and cover with 800 ml (27 fl oz) water. Leave to soak for 4 hours.

Strain the almond paste through a muslin cloth-lined sieve. Squeeze the cloth to extract the almond oils. Return the almond paste to the strained water and leave to soak for another 1–2 hours. Strain and squeeze again. Repeat the process once more if desired. Discard the almond paste.

In a medium-sized saucepan over low heat, gently bring the almond water to a simmer. Add the sugar and stir until dissolved. Remove from the heat and set aside to cool. Stir in the brandy.

Pour into a sterilized bottle or jar. This orgeat syrup will keep in the fridge for up to 3 months.

You can substitute hazelnuts, walnuts, pistachios or any other kind of nut to create delicious syrups that will add unique flavours to your cocktails.

HONEY SYRUP

makes 500 ml (17 fl oz/2 cups)

350 g (12½ oz) honey

In a small saucepan over medium heat, combine the honey with 250 ml (8½ fl oz/1 cup) water.

Gradually heat and stir until the honey is dissolved.

Pour into a sterilized bottle or jar. This honey syrup will keep in the fridge for up to 1 month.

For Rich honey syrup, use 700 g (1 lb 9 oz) honey, or halve the quantity of water.

VANiLLA SYRUP

makes 500 ml (17 fl oz/2 cups)

1 vanilla bean, split open and
   seeds scraped

440 g (15½ oz/2 cups) sugar
1 teaspoon vanilla extract

Place the vanilla bean and seeds with the sugar in a saucepan along with 500 ml (17 fl oz/2 cups) water. Bring to the boil over medium–high heat and stir until the sugar is dissolved. Stir in the vanilla extract and set aside to cool.

Strain into a sterilized bottle or jar. This vanilla syrup will keep in the fridge for up to 1 month.

CINNAMON SYRUP

makes 250 ml (8½ fl oz/1 cup)

3 cinnamon sticks   220 g (8 oz/1 cup) sugar

Lightly crush the cinnamon into pieces using a mortar and pestle. Transfer to a small saucepan along with the sugar and 250 ml (8½ fl oz/ 1 cup) water. Bring to the boil over medium–high heat, stirring until the sugar is dissolved. Set aside to infuse for at least 2 hours.

Strain into a sterilized bottle or jar. This cinnamon syrup will keep in the fridge for up to 1 month.

PASSiONFRUiT SYRUP

makes 100 ml (3½ fl oz)

100 g (3½ oz) sugar   pulp from 3 passionfruit

Place the passionfruit pulp and sugar in a small saucepan along with 100 ml (3½ fl oz) water and bring to the boil over medium–high heat. Stir until the sugar is dissolved. Set aside to and infuse for at least 2 hours.

Strain into a sterilized bottle or jar. This passionfruit syrup will keep in the fridge for up to 1 month.

VELVET FALERNUM

makes 750 ml (25¼ fl oz/3 cups)

2 tablespoons blanched
    slivered almonds
40 cloves, crushed
185 ml (6 fl oz/¾ cup) white rum
zest of 9 limes

8 cm (3¼ inch) piece fresh ginger,
    peeled and sliced
330 g (11½ oz/1½ cups) sugar
45 ml (1½ fl oz) freshly squeezed
    lime juice
¼ teaspoon almond extract

In a small dry frying pan over medium heat, toast the almonds and
cloves until the almonds are golden. Transfer to a medium-sized
sterilized jar along with the rum, lime zest and ginger. Shake vigorously
and leave to steep at room temperature for 24 hours.

Strain the rum mixture through a muslin cloth-lined sieve into a bowl.
Squeeze the muslin to get all the oils out of the solids. Discard solids.

In a clean sterilized jar, combine the sugar with 185 ml (6 fl oz/¾ cup)
warm water and shake until the sugar is dissolved. Add the rum mixture
along with the lime juice and almond extract and shake well to combine.

This velvet falernum will keep in the fridge for up to 1 month.

ORANGE BITTERS

makes 750 ml (25¼ fl oz/3 cups)

750 ml (25½ fl oz/3 cups) over-proofed vodka or rum (50% abv or higher)

250 g (9 oz) dried orange peel

1 teaspoon fennel seeds

½ teaspoon coriander seeds, lightly crushed

4 cardamom pods, lightly crushed

½ tablespoon gentian root powder (see note)

Combine the ingredients in a sterilized jar and seal. Store at room temperature for 14 days, shaking every second day.

Strain through a muslin cloth-lined sieve into small sterilized bottles.

This orange bitters will keep indefinitely.

Gentian root is the bitter root from the gentian plant. Available from health-food-stores or online.

If you'd rather not go to the trouble of making your own bitters, you can purchase flavoured bitters from good bottle shops and specialty liquor stores. Alternately, you can substitute Angostura bitters.

ALLSPICE DRAM

makes 750 ml (25¼ fl oz/3 cups)

250 ml (8½ fl oz/1 cup) white rum
35 g (1¼ oz/¼ cup) allspice
  berries, lightly crushed

1 cinnamon stick
155 g (5½ oz) soft brown sugar

Combine the rum and allspice berries in a sterilized jar and seal. Store at room temperature for 5 days, shaking every day.

On day 5, break up the cinnamon stick and add to the jar. Steep for another 7 days, shaking every day.

Strain through a muslin cloth-lined sieve into a clean sterilized jar.

In a small saucepan over medium–high heat, combine the sugar with 375 ml (12½ fl oz/1½ cups) water. Stir until the sugar is dissolved and set aside to cool.

Add the sugar syrup to the rum mixture and shake well to combine.

Leave the allspice dram to rest for at least 2 days before using. It will keep indefinitely.

PEARL DIVER'S MIX

makes 4 portions

20 g (¾ oz) unsalted butter, softened

45 g (1½ oz) honey

1 teaspoon Sugar syrup (page 250)

½ teaspoon Cinnamon syrup (page 255)

½ teaspoon Vanilla syrup (page 254)

½ teaspoon Allspice dram (page 259)

Mix the ingredients together in a small bowl.

This pearl diver's mix will keep for 1 month in an airtight container in the fridge.

COFFEE GROG BATTER

makes 4 portions

30 g unsalted butter, softened
45 g (1½ oz) honey
1 teaspoon Vanilla syrup
(page 254)

1 teaspoon Cinnamon syrup
(page 255)
½ teaspoon Allspice dram
(page 259)

Mix the ingredients together in a small bowl.

This coffee grog batter will keep for 1 month in an airtight container in the fridge.

DON'S MIX

makes 300 ml (10 fl oz)

100 ml (3½ fl oz) Cinnamon syrup
(page 255)

200 ml (7 fl oz) freshly squeezed
grapefruit juice

Mix the ingredients together in a small bowl.

Don's mix will keep for 1 month in an airtight container in the fridge.

cocktail index

Smith Street Books

Published in 2017 by Smith Street Books
Melbourne | Australia
smithstreetbooks.com

ISBN: 978-1-925418-33-0

CIP data is available from the National Library of Australia

Publisher: Paul McNally
Project editor: Hannah Koelmeyer, Tusk studio
Text: David Adams
Design and illustration: Heather Menzies, Studio31 Graphics

Printed & bound in China by C&C Offset Printing Co., Ltd.

Book 25
10 9 8 7 6 5 4 3 2 1